I0456462

CONQUERING THE SOUND OF A FAKING LION

WINNING SPIRITUAL BATTLES THROUGH THE POWER OF THE HOLY SPIRIT

H. A. BLAKE

Published by: H.A. Blake Publishing
In affiliation with Majestic Franchise Unlimited LLC
Pembroke Pines, Florida
Email: majesticfranc@gmail.com

FOREWORD

The voice blurted out, "They are waiting for mother and child to arrive, but it's going to be two coffins instead"!

- Before I was born, I already had a death sentence on my life!

ACKNOWLEDGMENTS

I would like to express my deepest gratitude to my Lord and Savior, Jesus Christ, for inspiring me to write this book. Your constant presence in my life has guided me through the ups and downs, and your unwavering love and mercy have shown me the true meaning of grace.

Thank you, Jesus, for filling my heart with your love and inspiring me to share your goodness with others. Your endless blessings and miracles in my life have given me the strength and courage to write about your amazing works.

I dedicate this book to you, Jesus, as a testimony of your faithfulness and compassion. May it be a light for others to see and experience your boundless love and mercy.

With all my love and gratitude,
H.A. Blake

CONTENTS

INTRODUCTION

When I started writing this book, I didn't know where to begin or what to write about. All I knew was that I had gone through some incredible things in life (I am still going through stuff as you read this book), especially when I came to know Jesus Christ of Nazareth as my Lord and Savior. These exceptional circumstances, along with a fascinating Christian journey (I got converted a while back) and the prompt of the Holy Ghost, had brought me to this decision. As a child of God, I have faced great challenges and fiery trials, but God brought me through them all. On this, I must emphasize that when you have signed up and enrolled in the army of almighty God, you must condition your mind with the help of the Holy Ghost so that whatever circumstances come your way will not break but empower you! Yes, this army is different. When going through tribulation, you must have that 'something great is coming out of this' attitude. Well, does that sound like preaching?!

Whether a person is a believer or not, as long as they exist in this life, they must preach to themselves, or else they will be trodden down or run over by some opposing entity trying to destroy their soul.

INTRODUCTION

So, while I was going through the motions, the Holy Ghost dropped the title of this book into my spirit. Yep, 'Conquering the Sound of A Faking Lion' was born out of adversity! This is a personal journey, a testament to the connection we can all have with God while we rumble through life's challenges.

Even though I got the title, as I said before, I didn't know where to start. Therefore, when the Holy Spirit reminded me of my mind-blowing past and present experiences with Almighty God and my life history from birth, it dawned on me what God's intention was regarding my life and destiny: [Jeremiah 29:11]. Indeed, His purpose for my life is more significant than my thoughts! Sometimes, one can never tell where God is taking them until they arrive. He will give you bits and pieces of the puzzle but never reveal everything. This unpredictability is part of the intrigue of God's plan. With that being said, please fasten your seat belt! He is about to take you on a wild journey to your destiny!

CHAPTER 1
THE THREAT BEFORE BIRTH

If you are a human being reading this book (of course, there is no alienated creature that existed on earth besides the Devil and his agents), I am telling you right now that you have just intended in your mind; if you've not already started, to defeat the Master of deception that plague and cause havoc in your life. My first encounter with the enemy of my soul was one summer (in my hometown and country, Jamaica) while I was asleep in an almost empty or incomplete room. This particular space we called an 'out room' was an extended part of the house and a cozy place to lay down and sleep undisturbed. Back then, I was just a teenager who didn't know who God was but knew something or just about enough about prayer and the Psalms of the Bible, taught to us (me and my brothers) by our mom.

It was almost midday or mid-afternoon when I tried to wake up but was unsuccessful! As seconds ticked away, which turned into minutes, I still tried to move my hands and feet, but to no avail! It was as if I was pinned down by a giant boulder stone or a crane or something! Despite this, I was very conscious in my mind. My brain sent signals to my whole being, but nothing happened. Even though I yearned to, I could not even open my eyes or make a sound. There I was, lying on my back, trying to battle an unknown but eerie force trying to prevent me from waking up! What was even more sinister was that I was pretty aware that this creepy and evil entity was trying to hinder my spirit from returning to my body! Sounds creepy indeed. But have no fear; you'll probably soon have your share of experience if you haven't already!

So, I was trying to wake up from my sleep, but I could not because of this evil thing pinning me down. The next thing I knew was that in my conscious mind, I started reciting the 'Our Father' nightly prayer that my mom taught me and my brothers from the Holy Bible when we were of a tender age. Yes, the mind is a powerful thing if you ask me. On that note, what are you using your mind to do right now? If it's something positive, your result will be fantastic. As I started reciting the words of this prayer that Jesus taught His disciples in my mind, "Our father which art in heaven, hallowed be thy name, thy kingdom come…" and before I could say, "For thine is the kingdom, the power, and the glory…" The overpowering force released me. As I looked back at that encounter with the forces of darkness, I realized that someone (any of my relatives) could have found me alone-probably dead on my back. But something about that prayer enabled me to overcome the wicked plot of the enemy. In the Bible, Hebrews 4:12 states:

> for the word of God is quick and powerful, and sharper than any two-edged sword. Piercing even to the dividing asunder of soul and spirit, and of the joints and marrow, and is a discerner of the thoughts and intents of the heart.

There is something about the word of God; using it with faith and authority will execute what it will.

Some inexplicable things convinced me I was born for adversity or spiritual battle. When my mother was pregnant with me, she received a death threat. You heard me right- a death threat was sent out against our lives even before I could exit the womb! That's awesome! I could say that now because overcoming such a feat (by the grace of Almighty God), I can look back and say, bring it on! Even though she didn't know the Lord and our savior, Jesus Christ, back then, my mom was threatened by an individual who was deeply involved in witchcraft. According to what I understood (from my mom, of course) was that my grandma was told that instead of a daughter and child coming back from the hospital, it would be two coffins! It sounds creepy, indeed. However, things didn't go well during her delivery.

You would probably think this is some form of superstition, but she went through one of the strangest ordeals in her life at the point of delivery. For hours, my mom was in labor and pain, even though the head of the baby was in the proper position for delivery. At one point, the midwives claimed that they couldn't find the head of the baby! It was a state of confusion mingled with the mysterious workings of the evil one. Nevertheless, by God's grace and mercy, she finally delivered. Thus, I can confess today that God is good; He has spared us for a reason. It's incredible how God watches our backs even before we acknowledge that there is a God! What an awesome God He is! If you are in prison right now (whatever prison it might be, whether physically or spiritually) for whatever reason, if you pause for a second and confess your sins, repent of them, and truly accept Jesus Christ of Nazareth as your Lord and Savior, then you will start to feel the power and presence of Almighty God enveloping and embracing your soul with supernatural love and peace! Wow! I felt God's anointing (the unction) as I penned this word of encouragement! Received Him Now! in the name of Jesus.

Growing up wasn't easy for me. More and more, I realized that life was a challenge, and I had to make up my mind to fight. I can vividly remember a point in time when I was around the age of five or six; my mom would put me on a transit bus (back home in the country where I am from, there was no such thing as school buses), and send me off to school in the mornings. Most mornings, the buses would be so jam-packed with passengers going to school and work that we would be all hot and sweaty when we reached our destination. There weren't many transportation options for certain people in the Caribbean islands. If you want to get where you are going less expensively and affordably, public transit is the one. And that is when you are at a certain standard of living. There were no other options except to walk.

So, it happened one morning when my mom put me on a super jam-packed transit bus. And being such a small to average kid, they squeezed me between a bunch of high school seniors. These were primarily high school females with their back parts pressing in on me from all sides! I was in the midst of a hot and airless space! Can you say claustrophobic? Well, I can't hear you! It was one of the most horrifying experiences I've ever had in my life. I thought I was going to die! Yup- who feels it knows it! I couldn't breathe properly, couldn't see anything at all, the air was so hot around me, and all I felt was the back parts of these females pressing in on me. I hollered and screamed all the way to my final stop for school. From that day onward, I never reencountered anything like it. That's because I told myself it would never happen to me again- like I am in charge!

Growing up, I could recall so many strange things; I may have run out of time. Being the eldest of four siblings, I was expected to be the pacesetter. When my mom was pregnant with me, she wished for a girl. I came out as a boy! Sorry, Mom, the plan wasn't yours. On that note, I must admit that I was forced to think each time (and chuckled to myself when I recalled her wish) what I would be like if her wishes were granted. Mark you, I am thrilled to confess that I am comfortable with my gender. Moreover, I am one hundred percent masculine! Thank God! In addition, I am strongly attracted to the opposite sex! Whew! … You can release your breath now if you were wondering where that was headed. I wanted to emphasize that I am just a simple man functioning and operating in my God-given attributes.

I could explicitly recall times when I could have died a million times over. Nevertheless, the Almighty God (El SHADDAI), who watches over the sparrows, was watching and still watches over me. He had often protected me, even when I didn't know Him. Some of my near-death experiences were from being mischievous and reckless to mere circumstances. I can recall one night; I was wrestling with friends on a porch back home in my country and ended up with a severe concussion. The wrestling intensified, and I fell over one of the columns and hit my forehead hard. The rest was history. It was a bloody situation. Another time, I was forced to hop off a moving transit bus, competing against each other to see who could get the most passengers. That afternoon, I ended up falling in the street with my khaki uniform torn at the knees, and one of the bus's rear tires narrowly passed my head! Fortunately, I didn't even break a bone- just a few bruises on my knees! Thank God! He was protecting me all the time!

The word of God declares:

> *For when we were without strength, in due time Christ died for the ungodly. For scarcely for a righteous man will one die: Yet per adventure for a good man, some would even dare to die. But God commendeth His love toward us, that while we were yet sinners Christ died for us.*

ROMANS 5: 6-9

Whew! I mention this scripture to show how great the love of God is towards every one of us- Adam's fallen race. Thus, I survived life's ordeal because of His love and mercy towards me. Let me ask you right now: has life been throwing punches at you lately? Call upon Jesus and watch the result! Remember this: you are exceptional in His eyes. When I surrendered my life to Jesus, I came to acknowledge how special I am to Him.

I know I could have died a million times over, but He was just there all the time protecting me. My only boastings today are His unfailing love, grace, and mercies toward me. Now that I know, I can always wear my Superman attire and say, "Devil, you are a liar"! Through Him, Jesus, who has given us the kingdom, we are more than conquerors! Amen to that! Throughout my life as an adolescent, I continue to face challenges. I have had friends who never left primary or even high school. I remember friends and schoolmates who never returned home to their parents. Some of those incidents were tragic, either by bus or motor vehicle. I even had a friend who went swimming in some dangerous river with other friends after school (on a Friday afternoon), got caught up in quicksand, and never made it out alive! His colleagues ran away and left him struggling. Eventually, they found his body the following week. With all that being said, it brought me to the point I want to make: I survived. I am still here! I overcame!

Now, do you think for one minute that I overcame so many challenges because of my skillfulness? I wouldn't believe you would dare, for I know it was because of God's grace, favor, and mercy on my life, coupled with a divine purpose that no one can explain except Him. So many times, things could have gone haywire, but instead, He allowed situations to work out on our behalf. When God has a purpose for your life, no devil in hell is big enough to stop it! I heard this saying before that no one can kill the purpose that God has orchestrated in your life- and I believed it. Everyone has a purpose in their lives. You who are reading this book have a purpose in life. Let me ask you, have you found your purpose yet? If not, stop now, take a minute or two to pray, and ask God what He wants you to do.

Interestingly, many of us haven't exited this world prematurely; why? Because we have a profound calling in our lives, and God would not allow it to happen until our mission here is accomplished. Yeah, please stop and think about it.

I grew up with two brothers (it was two then, and now I have three siblings), with me being the eldest. Our lives were very simplistic. We grew up in a humble home inherited from our great-grandmother to one of my (our mother's brother) uncles. My mother didn't have much but did her best to make ends meet. We often didn't know where the next meal was coming from.

Nevertheless, we trusted God that He would provide, and He did. I must point out that none of us was saved or even committed our lives to God back then. However, my mom used to have us kneel at the bedside every night to sing hymnals, read the Bible, and pray before we went to sleep. Not one of us would dare go to sleep without doing this ritual or even saying our prayer. Later in life, I realized this was inherited from my great-grandmother. Being the kind of strict individual she was, she would never allow anyone staying under her roof, whether permanent or temporary, to go to bed at night without saying their prayers. Yes, my great grandma was a strict one.

Living in that simplistic and humble home was sometimes a challenge for us. With the flooring being board, we had a cellar, and we would be plagued by what I would call 'creatures of the night.' Surrounded by many big and shady trees, our home would be prey to rats and ants. The rats would come and go, but the ants were more strategic. I think these ants were demonic back then (no pun intended). Some nights, we (my brothers and my mom) would take turns crushing these ants' heads as they shew up in droves continuously all night! These ants were like armies going to war. What was more bizarre was that, just like an army, they knew when to strike, and that was when everyone seemed asleep at night. Their heads were like the size of a standard pin. These giant red ants would just cut mercilessly into your skin with their relatively small but sharp, knife-like claws at both ends of their mouth! This would leave you in excruciating pain as you bled literally! We were often scared to close our eyes, much less to sleep. Yes, it is very creepy, indeed.

Anyways, trusting in God for our every need has helped us survive. Sometimes, we went to bed having just a piece of bread with sardines or 'tinned' mackerel. Nevertheless, we were grateful for life's seemingly small but significant things. When we were headed to school, our mom would make fried eggs and sliced bread for our lunch. Sometimes, it would be homemade 'roti' (baked or fried dough found chiefly in the Caribbean islands), potato, or cornmeal pudding. While some kids at school had the luxury of spending cash given to them by their parents, we could only afford our simple homemade meals. When the bell rang for a lunch break, we would humbly sit in class and eat lunch. There would be no time for embarrassment then. Who knew what that meant when you sat in class for so long and felt like your stomach was dropping out? However, there were times when mom would find herself with a bit of change, and then she would give us something to buy lunch. To sum it all up, I did enjoy my life growing up in primary school.

After graduating from high school, I didn't know what I wanted to do with my life. I didn't graduate with any subjects in GCE or CXC (these are standard examinations that prepare you for higher learning, university, or even the workforce environment). I had no guidance as to what I wanted in life. This was because my mom migrated during my early years in high school, and she was my biggest motivator then. Therefore, I didn't know where life was taking me. Then, I discovered that I could do reggae music. Not to say that I wasn't aware that I had this innate ability before- I didn't realize that I needed to improve on it or that it would benefit me in the future. I used to get up and write like there was no tomorrow. The content I wrote back then was cutting-edge. Everyone wanted to hear me spitting lyrics like it was no big deal. Dealing with the secular world, there was no rule regarding music- everything goes. I found myself writing lyrical content of all sorts. Some were humorous or funny, and some were not so humorous but promoted violence, sex, and marijuana usage.

However, I had a few from my lyrical genre that promoted spirituality. On that note, to be recognized as a talented reggae artist back then, an individual must have versatility. So not only were these contents spiritual, but they had such strong and positive vibrations that I had to look into myself and wonder if I was the one who wrote them. Then, I had a friend who was also interested in music. Coming from the same community and sharing some form of family connection, we both had a passion for reggae music. And so, becoming icons in our community, we were in hot pursuit to take the music industry by storm. With about four books of lyrical content under my belt, plus what I made up in my head daily, my vocabulary was up for any challenges that may come my way. There was a light pole on the street, just a few feet on a slope by my home, where my close friend and the community youths used to hang out and have fun. Many nights, we would be there spitting out lyrics at the top of our lungs while the youths around us would grab hold of anything they could use, such as buckets, old wash pans, etc., to create a beat or a rhythm. We did this almost every week. Some nights, even up to 2:00 am, we were still spewing out what we would call top-shot lyrics. Then, my brother (the one who followed me) became a promoter.

My brother and a friend of his started promoting stage- shows. These are concert-like events where young and upcoming reggae artists display their talents. My friend and I became increasingly popular as my brother and his business partner launched these so-called stage shows. Folks heard about us both far and wide as our popularity went viral. Reggae music was our first love, of course, and many times, we went to the extreme to prove it. We would be at our regular job all week, but at the weekend, we would try to find where the next 'dance hall' or party would be. Sadly, the little we earned from our so-called 9-5 job would only go up in smoke. We would spend it on liquor or booze that only lasted a few hours throughout the night.

Yes, this was our lifestyle- our god, and we knew and willingly embraced it. Compartmentalizing was what we were practicing without even realizing it. We believed there was a God, but like most people today, we were ignorant of His ordinance and His will for our lives. Our self-righteousness held us captive! We would confess to Christians when they approached us that we believe there is a God, and even debate with them that we knew Him, too.

Nevertheless, we never took the time to find out what He required of us. You see, my friend, believing there is a God is one thing, but knowing Him is another. Believing is just the beginning. It is like faith without works, which is dead faith! To be effective, both faith and work must operate together. Thus, believing and knowing who God is is paramount for eternal salvation.

Growing up in a society where everyone was uncertain of their fate was a big challenge. This is because we were all lost souls groping in the darkness! There was no sense of purpose or direction where we were headed. In other words, there wasn't any individual we could look up to as an actual role model. The order of the day is to find a way to survive- and it doesn't matter how. Reggae music was one of the popular routes to escape. Even if an individual doesn't have that innate ability to make music, they are likely to be successful if they try out of desperation! Yep, they could create a so-called hot topic, add some hot lyrics to it, or what's trending, and they would have gone viral. However, that one record would be their only thing; they can't surface with anything else for the next ten years. Nevertheless, they would have made a little money to help themselves. Indeed, the music was an escape route for almost anyone who wanted to make a quick buck!

Life could be as strange as a shape-shifting creature! I knew a particular individual I grew up with (from a younger age) who moved to another location with their parent, got the right kind of connection to the music industry, and became wealthy and famous through reggae music. This is life's lesson for everyone. You could be born in the most impoverished city, place, town, community, etc., and no one even knows your name, but that still doesn't decide your destiny. A proverbial term we use back home in broken English states: 'Man nuh dead nuh call him duppy' which means in proper English: 'If the man is not dead, then don't call him a ghost'! In other words, don't write anyone off! We often hear individuals speaking negatively about their families, friends, enemies, and themselves. They have already concluded the outcome of a person or a matter. However, God and time have often proven us dead wrong in our thoughts, words, and deeds.

God always has the final say in everyone's life. This is because it is He who made us, not we of ourselves. Thus, He knows the path we will take according to what's in our hearts, our reverence for Him, and our awareness of spiritual matters. Now, I am not saying that God is the one who decides our fate- it is the choice we make and the constant grinding that eventually propels us to our destiny. I didn't have a concrete sense of direction when I started doing music. One thing I know was that I was determined more than ever to burst out on the scene as one of reggae music's great giants. However, the God who knows the beginning from the end has other plans. A famous saying goes,

If you want to make God laugh, just tell Him your plans.

That's exactly what I was doing. Why God could only be God is that He is the only one I know that can bring about a good situation out of a bad one. I could say He turned my mess into a message!

With all of that, let us go into the story of my life. Shall we?

CHAPTER 2
THE CONVERSION

W hen an individual shows an extraordinary ability or skill in doing something far better than most of their peers, say, for example, in music, athletics, or cooking, etc., it is effortless for someone to point out that that particular individual has a special gift or talent. However, if that individual does not use this specific gift or talent to glorify God by, for example, serving others, then that gift or talent becomes worthless. I believe gifts and talents come from the Almighty God but are sometimes corrupted by the infiltration of evil and seductive influence. Everything that has ever been made or created must focus back on Him, from which all things derived. That said, I must suggest how I felt each time I attempted to perform on these stage shows or concerts. There were many times when I felt like something just wasn't right.

This was in the sense that although I hadn't converted to Christianity, at least not yet back then, I had deep thoughts, such as: "What am I doing with my life? Is this pleasing to God?" Or "If God should show up now, would I be in the right standing with Him?" All these thoughts kept creeping into my soul and gave me the thrills! Anxiety and uncertainty did kick in. Come to think of it, despite all the friends, families, and peers who cheered me on in my hot pursuit for wealth, fame, and stardom; there was a profound, intimate, and personal feeling regarding my creator that if I began to explain back then, no one would understand. Then something happened that turned my whole life upside down, inside out. As a reggae artist, I had a few intimate girlfriends. Yes, I said it right; quite a few intimate women were in my life. Back then, it was customary for a reggae artist to have many women. You probably got the picture already- it is called promiscuity.

However, a particular female was closer to me than the others. This was because I shared almost everything, I had with her. After a time, I wound up with her alone and inadvertently became a part of her family. Not very long afterward, she had an inexplicable and mysterious illness that almost cost her life. They took her to all kinds of doctors, but none could explain or even find a solution to her illness. She just had this nauseous and aching feeling in her stomach daily that wouldn't go away. Many folks around her (including close families) suspected that it was witchcraft. At one point, I visited her in one of her weirdest moments. She was lying down, looking very pale and sad, with her head resting in my lap. Then she began to sing- "one …, two…, three…, four…, five…, six…, seven…, I am on my way to heaven…" That's when it hit me that she was sending a clear message. I didn't know what to do, but we discussed going to church to find some healing.

The next thing I knew was that she visited a well-known church in our community near her home without my knowledge. I had to pass this church before I could get to her house. I remember hearing a voice distinctly speaking to me (especially whenever church was in session), saying, "Do you know you belong to this church?" I would fly past the church as if nothing happened! Don't get me wrong, I had gone to this church before when I was around twelve or thirteen. I was too young to understand some strange things that happened to me at the altar then. In other words, I almost got saved back then, 'tarrying' at the altar. However, news spread quickly among my peers (kids around the same age as me) in the community, saying that I was almost filled with the Holy Spirit. Knowing not how to handle this kind of situation at a tender age, I avoided visiting this particular church up to the point of my conversion.

Nevertheless, I have visited other churches even after that experience. Whenever folks invited me to their church, most of the time, I would show up. This was because I always tried to keep my promises and saw the house of God as a place of reverence. Deep within me, I always thought it was the right place to be, but I was always wrestling with the thought that I wasn't quite ready. Then I realized that God had the final say- worse if you were a chosen vessel. So, I visited her home that Sunday and understood that she went to church. A few hours later, heading home, I saw her little brother come charging up the slightly steep, sloped dirt road. With his voice chirping in excitement and a hilarious grin, he blurted out that his sister fell on the ground at church. I didn't know what took place then, but this little chap (he was the last of all her siblings, about five or six years of age back then) was grinning from ear to ear mischievously. Seemingly, he didn't understand what had happened, but he thought it seemed funny and dramatic. To see his compelling sister, who used to drag him up the hill to catch the bus for school, go down flat on the ground in a church was hilarious.

A few seconds afterward, she showed up behind him. The look on her face was worth a million dollars. It told me that something strange had happened. Her countenance was so calm and peaceful that it was tough to know that this was the same person who could barely walk (she was experiencing excruciating cramps in her stomach that were consistent and inexplicable) and was lying down with her head in my lap gulping about a week or so earlier. Then she broke the news. She was healed instantaneously and was filled with the Holy Ghost as the power of God moved mightily in a particular way at the church that day! Yes, I am talking about my then-so-called girlfriend who was very ill with some strange sickness and almost died. This was like an introduction to a new book about to open in our lives.

As I was heading back home that Sunday afternoon and pondering about what had just taken place with my then-so-called girlfriend, I looked up into the skies and found myself saying- "God, it seems like you trapped me now; you trapped me now, God." This resulted from my conversation with my then-girlfriend after her encounter with Almighty God. Seeing that God had stepped into her life, I asked her about her next decision, and she said it was up to me. I was a bit flabbergasted. I knew the decision she would make if I tried to break away. This was the severe part because I didn't want to be a stumbling block in her path, preventing her from embracing her new spiritual life.

On the other hand, I got the gut-wrenching feeling that God was working through her to get to me! So, with me using these words of being trapped, I knew I could not escape God's plan for my life this time. Moreover, the saints at the church encouraged her to invite me to church. This was because, after some thorough investigation, they knew she was in an intimate relationship with me. After all, this was a community where everybody knew everybody.

What made matters worse or better was that the church's pastor knew my mom and my family very well. As I hustled past the church that Sunday afternoon, she saw me. With a greeting of delightfulness, she echoed, "How are you? We've been praying for you, you know…Your mom and ourselves have been bruising off our knees for you to come to the Lord." She continued, "I am inviting you to church this Wednesday." Then, I knew God had set me up. I had no choice but to take the challenge. He who knew everyone's heart knew something was already occurring within me.

Moreover, it is Him who brings conviction anyway. So that night, I went to bed pondering about the day's event. Around midnight, no sooner as I was about to drift off, I envisioned a giant finger out of nowhere (like the index finger of an individual) coming down and abruptly touching me.

It was like about a hundred and twenty volts of electricity hitting my whole being! Immediately, I gave out a loud shout, and my entire body jerked violently from side to side. At the same time, my heart was racing in my chest. Fear got a hold of me for the rest of the night as I pondered what had just happened. Later in life, as I thought about it and told folks about my experience, I often joked that if there were a little bit more power in that finger, then it would have killed me. I woke up from my little sleep, thinking about my previous encounter. What's so funny is that I didn't even share my experience with anyone. This was because a cloud of conviction was hanging over me. I went to work, but it wasn't the same. At work, I wasn't speaking as much as I used to. All that time, my mind was occupied with the events that had led up to the moment. It was Ash Wednesday week, and this church usually had day and night services on Ash Wednesday at this time of year. However, other events were also taking place all over the country. The reason was that this was considered a public or national holiday. Thus, my friends and I had planned previously to attend a sports (athletic) event at a particular school not very far from where we lived.

I woke up that Wednesday with an urge not to go anywhere. All my mind focused on was the events that happened less than a week before. Even more interestingly, I had an uncle who lived (upon a little hill) about a stone's throw from where the church was located. I went by my uncle's house and lingered, curious about what was happening at the church. I could hear the singing of hymnals and the worshipping as the voices blared through the microphones. When I finally got to my friends, I told them I had no desire to go anywhere that day. I thought they went without me anyway. Then, the night came when I decided to visit the church as promised. Oh yes, it was like Nicodemus coming to see Jesus by night. My then so-called girlfriend was there also. Service was good in and of itself. The young man who preached (we were probably in the same age group) talked about a confrontation with a particular renowned religious leader at an airport and how he was rebuking him in the name of Jesus.

Then, services ended, and the preacher beckoned the unsaved to attend the altar. Without hesitation, my so-called girlfriend and I headed straight for the altar. Other unsaved individuals went also, but I could not recall because I was too focused. Now, the preacher began to ask, "Would you like to be saved" …as the microphone went from one mouth to the other. "Yes!" I uttered as the microphone reached my mouth. It was a complete assurance that shocked the onlookers. Of a certainty, they never saw it coming. Everyone's focus was now on me and my so-called girlfriend. Now, it was her turn to answer the question. Without a doubt, her answer was also a concrete 'yes'! Looking back, I wondered, "What if my answer was no? Then what would her answer have been seeing that the microphone reached my mouth first?" Notwithstanding, she did tell me that whatever my decision was, it would be hers also.

However, her way of thinking left me on dangerous ground! As I mentioned before, I wouldn't want to be the one standing in the way of an individual whom God is calling to Him. Now, I may be a sinner and 'wasn't saved,' so to speak, back then, and may have been ignorant of certain things about life in general, but I wasn't foolish regarding spiritual things! I had enough sense to know that God could remove everything and anything standing in the way of an individual He desired to bring to Him. Even up to this point, I've seen and heard testimonies of how God removed so-called idols or individuals who prevented His chosen ones from coming to Him. On this note, I must ask: "Are you standing in the way of anyone you know or are aware that God is calling?" We can be a hindrance in many ways, either directly or indirectly. With a live conscience, check carefully!

After the church heard our response, the preacher went to the pastor and muttered, "Your prayer has been answered." Then, certain saints who knew us and our family came directly to us and asked if we were confident about our decision. I knew with certainty that there was no other option for me. That touch that I experienced a few nights before had wholly transformed my mind and had messed up any rational or psychological thoughts I might have had regarding not accepting the Lord's calling!

One event after another, and there I was, the upcoming and promising reggae artist (renowned) poised to break out like wildfire, had just surrendered his life to God. Many didn't see it coming, no, not even myself. The following Sunday after Ash Wednesday, we (my so-called girlfriend and I) went down in water baptism in the name of Jesus Christ. It was early morning, in cold running water, just after sunrise. No doubt, some of my peers, friends, colleagues, and families showed up. For most of them, this came as a shock or a hard punch to the stomach. It probably was more potent than the touch I got a few nights earlier (pun intended). In one week, the life of their upcoming and promising reggae star has been changed!

I could recall seeing one of my peers, my closest friend's brother, breaking off two small pieces of dried sticks from a shrub that grew near the side of the river and racing them in the clean, cold, and clear water. It was a spirit of mockery. Yes, the distractions began, but I was too steel focused to regard them. As I was immersed in water, a great anointing came over me that caused my whole body to jerk violently from side to side. Sounds familiar? It was like the touch I experienced a few nights ago. It was like a new chapter started in my life.

I was very enthused about what was ahead of me. Though a few individuals couldn't come to grips with what had just taken place in my life, the joy and peace I experienced from being saved and the burden lifted from me was priceless. I went about minding my own business like nothing happened. Despite that, some individuals started monitoring us very keenly, especially me. Yes, the adversary started watching my every movement, scanning to see if there was any blot. At one point, there was even a rumor that I almost drowned when I was immersed in the water. This was because of the tremendous anointing that came over me as I was buried underwater. This came back to the holy scripture that declares that

> the natural man receives not the things of the Spirit of God, for they are foolishness to him. Neither can he know them because they are spiritually discerned

1 CORINTHIANS 2: 14

It is not good to be spiritually blind.

Over the following months of my conversion, I was given deadlines by my peers for when I would return to my old lifestyle. "Ouch!" It didn't happen. Thanks to Almighty God, who is my keeper and preserver. My former promoter even challenged me regarding my newly found Christian faith. He used to say things like, "I give you two weeks, three months," etc., to return to the world. As the time flew by and he realized that I was still holding on to my faith in God, He eventually backed down from his challenges. As I started this Christian journey, I began to stumble upon some deep and unfathomable truth that kept blowing my mind as I fasted, prayed, and studied the word of the living God, which is the Bible. Day after day and week after week, I passionately sought after him. In Matthew 5:6, the Bible declares:

> *Blessed are they which do hunger and thirst after righteousness: For they shall be filled.*

Then it happened one night, in the same place where I was lying down when I encountered the mighty hand of God. I went to bed feeling broken, disgusted and disheartened after struggling to live righteously. On this, I must assure you of the truth of the doctrine of the gospel that I have received. I was saved in an apostolic (or Pentecostal, if you may) church, meaning we follow the apostle's doctrine as stated in the Book of Acts of the Apostles [Acts 2:42]. This doctrine was initiated a few verses before [in Acts 2: 38] when
Peter stood up and pelted out the revelation of the salvation of Jesus Christ. This is the baptism in Jesus' name for the remission of sin and the receiving of the gift of the Holy Ghost. Now, I suggested all this to say that it is almost impossible to live for God without the grace and power that comes with the Holy Ghost to guide, protect, and keep us from the hour of temptation. Therefore, being 'waiting or tarrying' at the altar from Sunday to Sunday, week to week, month to month, and seeing nothing happening, I began to waver. Not that I chose to, but a tug-of-war was going on in my spirit; therefore, something had to give. So, there I was, lying there, knowing not what to expect next.

It had been approximately four months since I had been baptized and had been seeking the Holy Ghost, but nothing had happened. I thought of myself as being between a rock and a hard place. This night was my breaking point. However, how many of you knew that God would often show up when you reached the last end of the rope? Oh yes, He will, mark my words. So, I went to bed that night in tears of repentance and brokenness. Before bedtime, I took down a calendar hanging on the wall nearby, displaying a so-called picture of Jesus Christ, the Messiah. Yes, it was the Michael Angelo version for those of my readers whose curiosity got the better of them. Even Michael Angelo and everyone else will bow in the name of Jesus Christ of Nazareth. All I was focusing on was the thorn on his head and the nail prints in his hand. I looked at it attentively with great intensity (with tears streaming down my eyes), laid it on a nearby table, and went to sleep.

It was about 3:30-4:00 am when I woke up with my mind still focusing on the Lord and how I felt the night before. I reached out and grabbed the calendar, looked at it again, and then started to pray in my mind. It wasn't a long prayer, but I remember saying, "Let me speak, Lord, as I opened my mouth." I repeated this over and over in my mind. Thus, as soon as I opened my mouth, I was speaking to God in heavenly language! I was spitting out tongues that I had never spoken before! Hallelujah! It was like heaven came down, and glory filled my soul! I scrambled off the bed and went on my knees, scrambled back on the bed, and then off again (I didn't know what to do with myself), crying and laughing at the same time. Indeed, it was joy unspeakable and filled with glory. This time, unlike when the Lord reached down and touched me, I woke everyone up in the house. Indeed, the Holy Spirit came with a commotion- a noise abroad. I burst the door open, and the skies were red and looked more like blood. The rain began to drizzle as I looked up into the slightly overcast skies, praising and giving God glory.

As I headed to the passport office that morning, I was in a different world. The bus I took was jam-packed, but unlike other busy days, it was so quiet that you could almost hear the drop of a pin. Looking through the window, I could see that the rain was still slightly drizzling. There was also a slight flash of lightning and a peel of thunder now and then. However, I was intensely conscious of the inner peace I felt deep within me and how it caused me to feel like I was floating in thin air! In other words, at that moment in time, I felt like a feather floating. I felt like a king! Undoubtedly, I had a supernatural encounter with Almighty God. This sublime peace, joy, and love I experienced gave me a feeling that made me want to embrace the world. From that point onward, my life began to change drastically- for the better, for that matter. I started to fast, pray, and read the Holy Scriptures like there was no tomorrow.

As I mentioned in these proceedings in pursuing after Almighty God, I would like to inform the reader that being merely baptized in Jesus' name and being filled with the Holy Ghost does not necessarily mean reaching your destiny in God. I'll be frank with you that your journey has only just begun. Just after Abraham was converted (the Bible stated that God counted his faith and obedience for righteousness), He got up out of the company of his families and kindreds. He went to a place or country he had never been before. Eventually, he received a promise because of his obedience and trust in God. He was to be the father of all nations, and his offspring, like the sand of the sea and the stars of the skies, would enter into a land promised by God. Now, as it was in the natural, so is it in the spiritual. When we received salvation through Jesus Christ, we began a spiritual journey and eventually received eternal life. So, with all that being said, I started on this spiritual journey, not knowing what tomorrow would be. A spiritual lifestyle is not like a cakewalk or just another walk in the park. Instead, it is very much a supernatural and divine experience- a calling. However, a child of God would more or less likely encounter or experience situations and circumstances that they have never experienced before conversion! Fastened your seat belt.

CHAPTER 3
DEATH IS A BULLY

Being the only person who was baptized and filled with the Holy Ghost, I didn't grasp the fact or even come to the acknowledgment that I was like the watchdog over my family. I didn't even know the magnitude of the power of the Holy Ghost that came to live within me. However, Almighty God was about to prove Himself once again. It all started one night as I went to bed. I had a dream about my great grandma, who had been deceased a while back. She was lying on the bed, very ill, wrapped in white clothing from the crown of her head to the sole of her feet. I went by the bedside to embrace her, and she became like a baby in my hands. In the same dream, I noticed that the front door that led down the steps and out into the yard was slightly ajar. Then, I felt an opposing, intense, and eerie force approaching. As I glanced over my shoulder, I saw a tall, dark figure in a black felt hat, white and black striped suit, and a walking stick or crotch heading towards the door slightly ajar.

In an instant, the spirit of God lifted a standard, and I began to rebuke this evil and creepy-looking figure. I woke up the following day and found out that one of my little cousins (my uncle's baby boy) had fallen ill the night before. Now, being the only saved individual filled with the Holy Ghost in the entire family and a yard of three or more houses in one place, I knew I had work to do. I grabbed my uncle's baby, roasting with a high-pitched fever, and started praying for him. As I prayed for this precious little soul, I could sense the fever leaving his body as it cooled down against me. In addition, not only was he roasting with a high-pitched fever, but his eyes were sunken in his head, maybe because of the constant diarrhea that he was having. After praying, I returned him to his mom, who was a bit anxious. I then headed to work, returned home in the afternoon, and found out my little cousin didn't make it. After that, hell broke loose for five nights throughout my entire family!

The enemy of our souls decided to destroy the whole family, starting from small to great! Late the following Monday night, as everyone was asleep, I heard my aunt's baby father struggling in his sleep. It was as if he was trying to fight off some evil entity trying to pin him down. I jumped up suddenly as if I heard the sound of a war trumpet, ran over to where he was lying, and started pleading the blood of Jesus against that old dragon. Each time my uncle-in-law struggled to get up, grunting and fighting, this diabolical entity tried to press him back down on the bed! I forcefully continued to plead the blood of Jesus until he was released. My friend, using this kind of weapon for the first time, I can attest that there is power in the name of Jesus Christ combined with His blood! I burst the door open and chased that devil out of there! Then, the Holy Spirit drove me to pick up my aunt's baby girl lying between them on the bed. I began to anoint her with anointing oil (olive oil) that was kept nearby, speaking in heavenly language and covering her with the blood of Jesus!

In the meantime, my aunt rushed to the kitchen to retrieve a sliced lemon with salt (Traditionally, in Caribbean countries, they used this stuff to ward off evil spirits) and rubbed it on my uncle-in-law's face and upper torso. Immediately, the Holy Ghost drove me to knock on the doors of all my uncles and aunts and anoint all the babies found in their households with anointing oil in the name of Jesus. All these events took place in the wee hours of the morning while most neighbors were asleep. However, it took me a day or two to realize that I had entered an outright war (spiritual battle) with entities of darkness! Yes, my friend, it was a declaration of war! Being recently saved, baptized in Jesus' name, and filled with the Holy Ghost and fire, I had no clue that my Heavenly Father would already lead me into a spiritual battle!

From that point onward, right back to the following Friday, I was battling demonic entities. The Holy Scriptures declares,

> *No man can enter into a strongman's house and spoil his goods,*
> *except he will first bind the strongman; and then he will spoil his*
> *house.*

MARK 3:27

So, you see, as the only saved person filled with the Holy Ghost and the only strongman (in a spiritual sense) in this big entire household, I was a prime target. Mark you, I had a cousin back then who was freshly saved but wasn't filled with the Holy Ghost yet. Therefore, he couldn't partake in this fight. The enemy must first break down that robust defense system to reach his prey. Thus, the adversary would attack around midnight when I just dozed off. He would touch my legs with cramps (especially my left leg), trying to immobilize me. However, each night that he attacked, I would spring up out of my bed, pleading for the blood of Jesus and anointing my legs. This is because my legs would be feeling stiff, cold, and dead like they were on ice. This happened almost the same time every night until the following Friday. I would go to work in the morning, come back home, and prepare myself for spiritual warfare in the night.

Around midweek, it dawned on me that this wasn't just a mere or random attack. It did involve witchcraft for the most part. This or these entities were sent, but according to the contract they entered, they could not return until the work they were sent to do was accomplished. Their main target was my uncle-in-law. The reason was because of an altercation he had with another relative of mine. However, these dark forces couldn't take anyone from my aunt's household because that's where I lived. Each time the forces from hell attacked, I was up and ready, pleading the blood of Jesus, singing, clapping, shouting, marching up and down the pathways that led from the houses to the main street, up on the main Street, then back on the narrow paths to the houses again. This wasn't me of myself. This one thing I know is that it took the supernatural power of Almighty God for an individual to be up almost all night fighting spiritual battles, go to work in the mornings, and fast until around midday (practically every day of that week), return in the afternoon, and do it all over again during the nights for four days! I took zero credit for God's fantastic preservation!

During these nights of warfare, I didn't even know what the outcome would be like- all I knew was that a higher power was guiding me into victory. As the warfare intensified, I grew stronger and stronger spiritually, though my body was getting weary. There was one point when my close friend, whom I used to make music, asked me the next day at work (we used to work at the same place), after a night of an all-out battle against these wicked entities, if I was the only one marching, singing, and shouting the night before. He went further to say that it sounded like I had an army with me!

Knowing where he lived and that he could hear everything that happened over my side of the community, I knew he wasn't lying. No doubt I wasn't alone. Mark you, this guy wasn't converted- at least not yet, but he had to confess what he heard. Nonetheless, the warfare continued until the following Friday afternoon when the brethren from the church I attended decided to have a prayer meeting.

After the prayer meeting, the brethren from the church left, and everyone stood still, wondering what to do next. The gathering was good, yes, but I could still feel the presence of the forces of evil lurking around. Moreover, the Holy Spirit detected their every movement. When he slipped under one of the beds, I was charging at him and flipping the bed over! When he hid inside the closet, he was exposed. I eventually chased him out of our home once more through the blood of Jesus! Then the Holy Ghost turned my attention to my uncle-in-law, who was inside, sitting down and staring into space. I went over to where he was sitting and uttered in a low, firm, and steady tone of voice, "If you don't accept Jesus Christ as your Lord and Savior, you are a dead man." Instantly, my uncle-in-law sprang to his feet, like a bullet expelled from the barrel of a gun, and started shouting repeatedly, "Jesus! Jesus!" with his hands flung up. Immediately, I grabbed the bottle of olive oil and anointed his forehead in the name of Jesus Christ of Nazareth.

Without warning, his speech was changed, and he began to speak in unknown (heavenly languages) tongues as if he were made up of them! There went my uncle-in- law, who was sitting a few moments earlier fretting himself to death (because of these determined entities that wanted to take him out), pacing the floor back and forth, shaking his hands in a fist-like manner and with a wide grin on his face shouted in broken English, "ah suh Jesus sweet?! Ah suh Jesus sweet?!" Repeatedly. To me, this was the greater part of the warfare! This was the victory phase! Before my very eyes, I saw a mouse transformed into a lion! To God be the glory! Great things he has done. Hallelujah! Despite being exhausted from almost a week of spiritual battle, I was shouting and rejoicing. I could feel the whole environment changed. The atmosphere became enlightened by the awesome power and presence of the Almighty God. At that very moment, I knew that the adversary had been defeated. I could overhear myself saying, "Death, where is thy sting?! Grave, where is thy victory?!" The Holy Scriptures declares in 1 Corinthians 15: 54 that death is swallowed up in victory. In other words, God has trod on death and hell and has come through for his people again.

The following day, my uncle-in-law started laying down rules and protocols around his household, which sounded familiar. He was like, "I don't want any smoking, drinking, or word cursing around here." Everyone was amazed by this man's transformation. However, these rules and protocols didn't last long. Not even for two weeks, for that matter- for before long, he returned to doing the same thing he prohibited. You see, my friend, I realized after many experiences and being with the Lord for a long time that the quick run doesn't cut living for Almighty God. He had not surrendered his life to God. The Christian lifestyle is a journey, and there are no shortcuts on this road! What you see is what you get. That is it!
Jesus told His disciples,

> *If any man will come after me, let him deny himself, and take up his cross daily and follow me.*

LUKE 9:23

Christian living It's not just simply a walk in the park.

One of the weapons that the enemy uses to try and destroy us all is the fear of death. Yes, you heard me right- almost all of humanity, at some point in their life, had feared death! The enemy used this tactic to jerk the very core of our souls and emotional beings. This is because many individuals think that when a person dies, they cease to exist. However, that is not the case eventually. The Holy Scriptures tell us in many instances that God will cause all the dead to get out of their graves: [John 5:25, 28]. Yes, He will bring back to life every living soul to be judged and then sent to their eternal abode, whether it be eternal heaven or hell. Thus, the soul, which is the inner man and the core of a human being, can never cease to be in existence. "Why?" Remember, in the book of Genesis, God blew His breath in a dust-formed man, and he became a living soul. That part of God that he breathed into the dust-formed man cannot die but ever in existence! Do you get the picture now? So then, when the dust is no longer inhabitable, the soul must evacuate! Thus, the dust-formed man returns to the dust, and his soul returns to the one he came from, God. Oh, what an awesome God!

The soul- the blueprint of our existence, is definite and unique. This soul will take on a new body that can no longer die [1 Corinthians 15: 51-55]. Knowing this fact, saints and friends, we ought to decide while we are still alive, and the blood is still flowing through our veins which pathway or road we will choose- the one to eternal life or eternal damnation. Now, with all that being said, let us go back and see why the adversary sometimes uses death to drive fear in the lives of humanity and why God desires us to be fearless. Ever since we were born and even long before then, men have been dying (the first man to experience physical death was Able. [Genesis 4: 8] However, the adversary of our soul would want us to think that everything stops here and that there is no hope for an individual who dies to come back to life again. He had been using these lies for centuries. The word of God says that my people are destroyed for lack of knowledge because they have rejected knowledge. [Hosea 4: 6]

The result of this rejection breeds hopelessness, which causes those who are victims to fear the future and the unknown. However, unlocking the mysteries of Godliness will cause an individual to overcome them by conquering the sound of the faking lion- the devil. Salvation in Jesus Christ brings light and righteousness. When you accept this full and free salvation, God's righteousness will flood your whole being. Eventually, fear and hopelessness begin to fade away. In the book of the Psalms, David declares:

Yea though I walk through the valley of the shadow of death, I will fear no evil:

PSALM 23:4

Death is a bully! if you are fearful, he will get the better of you! Hence, our Heavenly Father prompts us occasionally to fear not. Countless times in the Holy Scriptures, God repeated that we should not fear.

Furthermore, the Bible states that fear breeds torment. Now let me ask: has your mind been constantly plagued by real or unreal fear? Well, I command you to snap out of it! In the mighty name of Jesus Christ of Nazareth!

Fear of the unknown has gripped humanity since Adam and Eve's generations came to understand and embrace the knowledge of good and evil. Sin has cast a shadow of hopelessness over humanity that causes misery, restlessness, and a fearful tomorrow. Many lion-like sounds are roaring all around, trying to intimidate the people of God. Can you detect the sound of a faking lion? Will you submit and run away? Or will you be bold and stand your ground in the name of Jesus? This is where the armor of God should be displayed. Without the whole armor of God, it would be impossible for us to win the victory.

You see, my friend, in this present day and age, living as a warrior for Christ, we still must face 'the strong bulls of Bashan along with the Beast of

Ephesus.' We cannot afford to be cowered because of the bluffing of the adversary. Let us quit ye like men and be strong. God is depending on us to be faithful- Even unto death. Are you willing to go all the way with Him? There is no other way to be victorious but through Jesus Christ- the lamb slain from the foundation of the world. If you are fearful today, there is a solution- God is the answer. Whatever situation you may be facing, the solution remains the same. The devil's tactics is to intimidate and bring us under subjection.

Today, many folks are afraid to die simply because they do not know where they are headed. If, for example, my readers, you didn't know better, wouldn't you think there's got to be a solution for your mind-boggling question of "where do I go when I die? And where do I find the answers to life's critical questions?" Well, the Bible has the answers! I drew this scenario because many people have these questions but sadly reject where to find the solutions- the Bible. If I hadn't proven the Bible to be the word of God, I wouldn't have been writing this way. However, my deep and intimate experience with Him helps boost my confidence in His word.

God cannot deny Himself, and that's one of the reasons why the Pharisees, Sadducees, and Scribes had a hard time figuring out who Jesus was! They could not believe that the God of their forefathers, Abraham, Isaac, and Jacob, would appear on earth in the manner He did- though it was written in their Holy Scriptures. This brought us back to what the Scripture said about faith:

> But without faith, it is impossible to please Him: for he that cometh to God must believe that is, and that He is a rewarder of them that diligently seek Him.

HEBREWS 11: 6

Abraham started by having faith in God. We should also follow suit. There is no other way to approach Him than what He requires. Too many people seek to know God and approach Him inappropriately.

When we conjure up our thoughts and philosophy about knowing God, we open the doors to deception. This is one reason we have so many different religions today. Many went and carved their gods (sometimes through misunderstanding), bowed down, and worshiped the same. However, Paul told the Athenians (Of Greece, Athens) that they were too superstitious. In other words, they need to know who the Real God is:

> Then Paul stood in the midst of 'Mars hill,' and said, Ye men of Athens, I perceive that in all things ye are too superstitious. For as I passed by and beheld your devotions, I found an altar with the inscription, To THE UNKNOWN GOD. Whom therefore ye ignorantly worship, he declares I unto you. God that made the world and all things therein, seeing that He is Lord of Heaven and Earth, dwelleth not in temples made with hands; neither is worshipped with men's hands as though He needed anything, seeing He giveth to all life and breath and all things;

> And hath made of one blood all nations of men for to dwell on all the face of the earth, and hath determined the times before appointed, and the bounds of their habitation; that they should seek the Lord if haply they might feel after Him, and find Him, though He is not far from every one of us: for in Him we live and move and have our being.

ACTS 17: 22-28

When an individual does not have the light of God shining within, he will be ignorant of every spiritual thing concerning God. He would even find himself fighting against God and things related to Him. Eventually, he would become fearful of his future and what lies ahead.

When the light of God shines into your whole being, it's like a new day is dawning. Your entire perspective of life is changed, and everything about you starts to adjust to the will and purpose of God for your life. Eventually, you begin to be transformed into his likeness as your mind is renewed daily.

No one ever came to Jesus and be the same! Yes, individuals may return to their old ways, but the faithful few who stick and stay with God move on from dimension to dimension and from glory to glory! Hallelujah! I can only describe it as God on the inside working on the outside! Amen.

The experience of God in an individual's life eventually causes them to become fearless. For things that used to make us afraid, the Lord commanded us to 'fear not!' for fear brings torment. Another Scripture declares:

For God hath not given us the spirit of fear; but of power, and of love, and a sound mind.

2 TIMOTHY 1: 7

Now let me ask: what are you afraid of today? Are you scared of dying? Jesus said He is the resurrection and the life. That tells me that if I die in Jesus's name, I die with resurrection power! Furthermore, I am not dead but asleep! Wow! Isn't that some awesome stuff?! Many do not want to die, but in the last few days, the Bible stated that the evil men of the Earth are going to seek death (when God's judgment rains down on the inhabitants of the Earth), and death will be fleeing from them!

And the fifth angel sounded, and I saw a star fall from heaven unto the earth: and to him was given the key of the bottomless pit. And he opened the bottomless pit; and there arose a smoke out of the pit, as the smoke of a great furnace; and the sun and the air were darkened by reason of the smoke of the pit. And there came out of the smoke locusts upon the earth: and unto them was given power, as the scorpions of the earth have power.

And it was commanded them that they should not hurt the grass of the earth, neither any green thing, neither any tree; but only those men which have not the seal of God in their foreheads. And to them, it was given that they should not kill them, but they should be tormented five months: and their torment was as the torment of a scorpion when he striketh a man. And in those days shall men seek death, and shall not find it; and shall desire to die, and death shall flee from them.

REVELATION 9: 1-6

Now we can see why the Most High God told us not to fear because He controls everything, and nothing controls Him! Indeed, death has no terror for the blood-washed saints! Let's go spiritually, shall we?

CHAPTER 4
GOD IS SOVEREIGN OVER ALL POWERS

As mentioned in the previous chapter, my uncle-in-law returned to do the same thing he told everyone else not to do around his household when he was filled with the Holy Ghost. The problem with that was that Almighty God would not let this great deliverance (His undeserving grace and mercies) that he had wrought in the lives of my family go unnoticed. God will not give His glory to another. No sir! Neither will he leave any task or work that He begins in us unfinished. With that, my uncle-in-law was filled with the Holy Ghost (this is confirmation, according to God's word, that gift and calling come without repentance) to rescue him from the peril of the enemy. It wasn't of his own will, but God saw it feasible to fill him with power to ward off the adversary. However, my uncle-in-law's duty was to follow the protocols for complete deliverance by repenting, confessing his sins, and accepting the Lord and Savior by baptism in His name. He ignored all this and continued with his old lifestyle.

Then it happened one night as we were all asleep. God allowed the entities to return. Although they couldn't destroy anyone this time (my uncle-in-law was filled with the Holy Ghost despite his reluctance to obey God's word for his life, and now he is responsible for his household), he tormented the whole household almost every night. My uncle-in-law would get up in the middle of the night to assist me in fighting off these evil forces that were trying to destroy us while we slept. At this point, I was unaware that it was God's will this time for it to happen. Being a very stubborn individual with a sense of ingratitude, my uncle-in-law forgets what God has done for him.

Now, his whole household was in jeopardy! But come to think of it, how many times had God delivered us from all kinds of dangers and destructions, and we got up the next day or a week or so and forgot what He had done? If we are honest enough, we can all say we are guilty.

Nonetheless, God knows exactly when and how to touch our weak spots to remind us! No matter how straightforward and trivial the thing He had wrought in our lives seems, we should give Him the glory and honor due unto His name. So, this attack continued night after night till my uncle-in-law sought help outside of God's source- that is, help from a witch or a wizard. Big mistake. That night, he came in with a few bottles of vials and laid them down on the top of a Chester drawer in the room where he sleeps. This time, when we went to bed, the warfare intensified. The enemy began to touch my feet, trying to immobilize me with cramps. As Usual, I sprang up, pleading for the blood of Jesus and anointing my feet. Then the Holy Spirit led me to where these vials sat on the Chester drawer. With a sweep of my hands, I snatched them off and cast them into one of the pitched dark gullies on either side of the house. Nights after that, we could still smell the eerie odor from the gully, rising even after the rain fell.

Despite all this, my uncle-in-law still decided to hold on to his old lifestyle. Then it came to the point that we all had to clear out of the house, every single one of us, man, woman, and child. The whole place was saturated with demonic entities. We evacuated one night over to my grandma's house next door. I vividly recall seeing my uncle-in-law standing on my grandma's verandah, looking at his home, saddened and disheartened. That night, over by our new shelter, I tried to sleep but to no avail. I was traumatized by the chronological events that led up to this moment. A sudden thunderstorm worsened matters as I tried to lie down and sleep. As I lay down, the flashes of lightning and the crashing of thunder reminded me that God had seen everything and was displeased with my uncle-in-law's rebellion- and even the whole family in that case. Then, the next moment, my mind drifted back to the Bible when Moses was trying to bring the people of Israel to know their God. Nonetheless, many were stubborn and reluctant. Thus, God brought His judgment on them time and again.

After this last ordeal, my uncle-in-law finally decided to surrender his life to Almighty God. He requested to be baptized the following Sunday without hesitation. Now, on this, let me take the time to ask you, if you are not already saved (baptized in the name of Jesus Christ and filled with the Holy Ghost and fire), what would it take for you to surrender all and come to Jesus? Would it have to take some tragic circumstances, such as sickness, death, deprivation, etc? I hope not. As I said before, I will say again that when you are chosen, and God has His eyes on you, He will do everything possible to bring you to Him. He would even go to the extent to touch you where it hurt most! That said, wouldn't it be better to run to God when His arms are wide open than when his anger is kindle? Who can stand before Him once He is angry? So, we see that it's far better to fall and the rock and be broken than the rock to fall on us and grind us to pieces.

The following Sunday night after the baptism, my uncle slept like a baby in his bed! Once more, God delivered a rebellious house! Eventually, these demonic entities crawled out in shame, one after the other. Glory be to God! Who can fathom God's grace and mercy; For a broken and a contrite heart he will not despise. He can pull us out of trouble, even when we are in our sinful conditions. Not one, not two are, or three times, but as many as it takes! Way too often, we choose to run away from God into the path of destruction, but as always, His love and patience bring us right back to him. My uncle-in-law knew the right thing to do. However, he chose to stay away from the One, who is a shield and protection from danger. When everything is done and over with and the smoke is cleared, we can think back and say, if we'd only known. Nevertheless, Almighty God is always ahead of us and everything else.

Countless times, especially in the book of the judges in the Bible, as soon as Israel repented of their sins, God caused them to overcome their enemy. Who can fathom God or the patience of the Almighty? God's patience, by and in itself, is absolute power! the Bible states that

> because sentence against an evil work is not executed speedily, therefore the heart of the sons of men is fully set in them to do evil.

ECCLESIASTES 8:11

The sooner an individual becomes conscious of who they are and the purpose of their existence, the better it is for that individual. We came into existence to do one and only one thing: to serve and worship Almighty God. Anything else outside of this scope is devilish. That was the very same reason why Lucifer was cast out from the presence of God. He left his purpose (which is to serve and worship God) and became a narcissist. We cannot make one strand of the hair on our heads black or white (even if you dyed it, it won't be permanent!), so the whole duty of man is to fear God and keep His commandments.

No one will ever understand or even fathom anything about life beyond this one until they encounter the spirit world. A wise and intelligent warrior learns his opponent's tactics and uses them to counter and eventually defeat them. It has been said that to stop the approaching of a grizzly bear, one must push the shoulders upward and the chest outward to appear big, which will cause the creature to back up. Well, there is no doubt about it: the enemy of our souls uses this tactic on simple and ignorant individuals almost every day of their lives. If we know the opponent's strategy against us, we are one step away from victory! First of all, a spiritually matured child of God acknowledges that they do not fight against their flesh and blood but principalities and powers, the ruler of darkness of this world, and finally, spiritual wickedness in high places.

Where and how do we get weapons to fight against these entities? Returning to the Bible, we would realize that spiritual things existed before the natural. Thus, God called all things from the spiritual into the natural. When humans (Adam and Eve) fell from their first estate or state of being, they lost all access and authority to the spirit world. This meant that despite their still having the image and likeness of God, they no longer had the power to rule or execute authority. This was one of the reasons he had to leave the paradise garden. Sin began to reign over man; thus, humanity was subject to principalities. However, the second man, Adam (Jesus, God manifest in the flesh), came to restore man and put him back into his rightful place. When Jesus uttered 'it is finished' that day on the cross, the spell or curse was broken off the life of man, and now we can be restored via way of the cross and the shed blood of the ultimate sacrifice for sin, which is the lamb of God. Wow! Isn't that awesome? Those of us who have experienced the matchless love of God can attest.

The most brutal blow to the kingdom of darkness came when Jesus rose again. The Devil received a sucker punch, hell trembled, and every screeching abject scampered away at the sound of his footstep as he approached hell's gate to get his captives out of there!

After Jesus arose, he brought this to the disciples' attention, saying that he had given them power over all the enemy's power. Thus, the faking lion has been defeated! Hallelujah! However, many of us have not acknowledged this yet. Why? Because it can only be manifested or proven by obeying and exercising God's word through faith. Therefore, fighting a spiritual battle with physical or natural weapons is impossible. It would be an ineffective and worthless effort. Imagine someone under a spiritual attack and grab a machete or even a firearm. It would be useless. Firstly, they cannot see what they are fighting; secondly, a spirit does not have the physical characteristics of a human, though they may temporarily have access to a body.

So now we see that from the fall of Adam, the adversary of our souls took advantage of humanity up to the point of Jesus rising from the grave. This is because we were ignorant of his devices and, more so, didn't have what it takes to fight back. Sadly, even up until this day, many are still victims of Satan's heinous plot and scheme simply because they are still in the valley of the dead (spiritually dead) and know not what befell them. If you are a born-again, blood-washed child of God reading this book right now, I must inform you that we have work to do. Hell gates must be stormed, and captives must be set free! Firstly, we must thank God for the individuals who likewise were praying for us to be loosed from the wicked grip of the enemy, and we should, in turn, pray for others to be set free.

The Bible tells us that

the weapons of our warfare are not carnal but mighty through God
to pull down strongholds

2 CORINTHIANS 10:4

To effectively defeat the adversary, we must practice warfare! Training camps or boot camps (consecration, prayer fasting, and studying the word of God) must be set up. Jesus did everything for exemplary reasons. After being baptized by John the Baptist, he headed to the wilderness, stayed there, and fasted for forty days and nights. He then headed back into town, filled with power and authority!

Notwithstanding, He could have brought with Him all the powers of heaven, but His actions were an example for us to follow as humans. When Jesus told his disciples that he had to go for the Comforter to come, He ensured that we were equipped for the task ahead. This Comforter eventually came on the day of Pentecost and is still active in the lives of the Believers today:

Then Peter said unto them, Repent, and be baptized everyone of you
in the name of Jesus Christ for the remission of sins, and ye shall
receive the gift of the Holy Ghost. For the promise is unto you, and
to your children, and to all that are afar off, even as many as the
LORD our God shall call.

ACTS 2:38-39

Now, being filled with the Holy Ghost and fire, man has access to the spirit world! The disciples now have the power to cast out demons, heal the sick, raise the dead, etc., just as Jesus told them. The weakest of the saints can now bind legions of demons and cast them down to hell's belly. Oh, what a work God did wrought on Calvary's cross! It's imperative that every human being on this face of the earth learn the art of spiritual warfare. We must learn how to fight to preserve our salvation to inherit eternal life. Believe it or not, being baptized and filled with the Holy Spirit is the beginning of preparation for a lifetime of spiritual battle. Jesus told his disciples that if any man should come after him, he should deny himself, take his cross, and follow me daily. Yes, my friend, the war is on. The spirit world of darkness was having a field day before salvation came; now it is time for us to have a field day, shaking the very foundation of hell and moving it out of its place through the power of the Holy Ghost!

God is present everywhere. However, the children of God often forget this fact when faced with dire circumstances. We (those of us who have been baptized in Jesus' name and received the Holy Ghost) should be aware that the presence of Almighty God filled the whole universe infinitely! Nothing exists without His presence or knowledge. This may sound too powerful and profound to many reading this book, but it is simply the truth and the fact to those who are enlightened. Let's take, for example, the extensive vast and open skies, or the firmament above. Has anyone gone anywhere in this world where no sky is hanging overhead? If your answer is no, then you are correct. So, if God created the heavens stretched across the universe so there is no end, wouldn't you think that the creator Himself is much more magnificent?

Now, if Almighty God is so much more significant, can anyone escape His presence? And if His presence is everywhere, wouldn't you believe He sees and knows everything? No offense here, but I would think that a rational and intelligent individual would agree. The physical, combined with the spiritual things, constantly manifest God's glory. On this note, we can attest that Almighty God rules, controls, and monitors both the spiritual and physical realms. Whatever is spoken or executed in the spiritual realm will be manifested in the physical realm. Most individuals may not know this, but the spiritual and physical realms interact periodically. This is why a child of God must call those things that are not as if they were! God has given man this kind of authority from the beginning of time- and that was when He decided to make man in His image. No wonder the Holy Scriptures declare that we are gods: [Psalm 82:6]. Thus, the god- ship status didn't occur after the Fall, as Satan has suggested to Eve, but this god-ship status was ingrained in the very blueprint of man when God formed him out of the dust and blew breath into him. The sovereign God decided for man to be as close to Him as possible, and for that cause, He made man in His image and likeness.

Now, with this title being placed on humanity, it doesn't mean that we are our own Gods or should intrude or even trespass on that Holy platform of sovereignty solely confined to Him! Remember that that same circumstance brought Lucifer's (now called Satan) downfall. We should always be conscious and acknowledge that He, God, is our Superior, and unlike Him, we are subject to certain limitations. We should not think of ourselves more than we ought to. King Saul, the first king of Israel, started very well, with right standing, both with God and man. But somewhere along the way, he got caught up with himself and the status of his position. His narcissistic behavior eventually cost him dearly. He failed miserably, costing him the throne and his son's life.

However, executing and operating in our God-given jurisdiction is best-fearing the One who has given us such authority. This is the only way we can conquer the sound of a faking lion! Sounds can be terrifying- especially if it is an uncertain one. However, some sounds are distinctive, so we can easily recognize them. Now, some sounds can be mimicked, which is where the problem arose. Some mimicking sounds seek to entrap, deceive, or intimidate their prey. Now, because our God is sovereign and is not governed by space, time, or matter, we can rest assured that He can take care of the deceptive and constant roaring of the adversary whose intention is to intimidate us daily. He is the God that dwells above and beyond natural existence.

The Psalmist David discovered that there was no way he could escape from the presence of God [Psalm 139:7]. The presence of God filled the whole universe- He is just there all the time! In other words, He had nowhere to go! Because God is a Spirit and the Creator of all things, including man, our finite mind can't seem to fathom or grasp how Almighty God would be All present, All-powerful, and All-knowing simultaneously! We can safely think that this was probably one of the factors that caused Lucifer to fall significantly from his heavenly status. Blood-washed saints of God can't afford to underestimate the magnitude of God's sovereignty and greatness! We can't sever Him from or exclude Him from any portion or part of our lives, or even the universe, for that matter! To sum it all up, at the end of the day, we simply can't get rid of Almighty God! Ignorant and impertinent men speak proudly and loftily about things they do not understand because of arrogance. Nevertheless, God is patient with all, not willing that any should perish but that all should come to repentance. God's attributes and character would not allow Him to cut man off without a fair trial.

So now that we observe how God reigns supreme, we should fear and honor Him for who He is and His goodness and mercies toward us. Scriptures state that the eyes of the Lord are in every place, beholding the good and the evil. In other words, nothing is hidden from His eyes. You may be wondering now why, when facing certain situations in life, it seems as if God isn't there. Well, my answer to that is this: God is not in a box or a trinket, so we could wave a wand or make a particular sound, and He will pop out just like that. He is the sovereign God who answers to no man but will respond according to His will and our right standing with Him. Yes, my friend, I said it right- According to His will and our right standing with Him.

It doesn't necessarily mean He was not there just because we didn't get a particular response from Him during our trials. He will choose to answer or not to answer in His way and His own time. However, we will be disappointed if we anticipate Him answering us when we want Him to. Nevertheless, He is always on time! Isn't that awesome? God says: "I got this; you don't know like I do!" Almighty God always finds a way to impress us with who He is. So often, we limit God and worry about the slightest matter. Then He would swoop down, step in, and make it seem like the problem wasn't there in the first place. What an awesome God He is! In the book of Isaiah, the Lord spoke to the prophet, declaring:

> *Ye are my witnesses, saith the Lord, and my servant whom I have chosen: that ye may know and believe me, and understand that I am He; before me there was no God formed, neither shall there be after me. I, even I, am the Lord; there is no savior beside me.*

ISAIAH 43:10-11

God doesn't need help or advice from anybody! The creator of the universe can handle all things simultaneously without a blink of an eye. What kind of God is this? One of the biggest mistakes one could ever make is to think that God could be limited! He proved Lucifer wrong when he cast him down with one-third of heaven's rebellious angels. They thought they could have prevailed against the supreme being who hides Himself, and His ways are far past finding out! [Isaiah 45: 15]. Until an individual comes to know the God who created the heavens and the earth, he will always be deceived by the devil and his bunch of thugs. Without the Light shining in us and the spiritual eyes popped open, we'll be raw meat for these faking beast-like entities! As long as the enemy can prevent us from knowing or coming to the Truth (Jesus is the Way, the Truth, and the Life), we would be like strange creatures groping in the darkness without hope or any sense of direction. Remember, these entities have nothing to lose! They already knew what time it was the minute they were kicked out of heaven's congress and God's headquarters. The power Lucifer was left with became a snare to him and his entities. Kudos! - To Almighty God, for He reigns forever, and who can stand against Him? Hallelujah!

CHAPTER 5
DOES LIFE MAKE ANY SENSE?

Many of us couldn't care less about the life we are living now, while others only care about what will happen next or what the next day has in store. But have you ever thought about why or for what purpose we existed? Indeed, we were not always here. That means that we came from somewhere, and it is a surety that we are headed somewhere. One of the laws of science is that there is a reaction for every action. The only logical and truthful concept about this is found in the holy scriptures. The Bible speaks about a unique and supreme being that made all things in heaven, earth, and the universe. So now that we have a Supreme Being in the picture, it would be logical that human beings came from Him, right? Now, it came back to the question: why are we here?

I was like a little kid in a candy store when I found out! Let me put it this way: my excitement was more than popcorn in a microwave! God made all things, including humans, merely for His pleasure! That's it! There we go! Still not excited? Here is the kicker: God pulls gods (humanity) out of His bowels so that they can enjoy Him and the things that belong to Him! Firstly, I thank God for life and my very existence. Now I give God all the honor and glory due unto His name for the great work He wrought for us on Calvary. [Isaiah 63: 5, Acts 20:28] If we forget anything else, let us remember this: the soul is still alive even when the carcass (the body) returns to earth. This assures us that the soul goes back to God and is kept in reservation for their final destination- eternal redemption or eternal hell. We'll be forever joyful if we trust Him and follow His commands. If we go against the grade, it is everlasting punishment! There is no cut, no corner about this deal. It is straightforward, no in-between.

Further, we could look at it this way: it's like a traffic light without the amber. Thus, there are only two choices, either red or green. Now you got the picture. Now, I say all this to say that despite God's desire for all to be saved, sadly, many will miss out on this complete and free salvation. "Why is that so?" One would ask. Well, 'free will' is the answer. God has given us Power, Authority, Intelligence (PAI), and free will. Now, like a goat, we could take our PAI along with our free and go roaming all over the place and end up in the belly of a wild beast or over a precipice (the devil and hell), or we could be like a sheep that adheres to certain boundaries and restrictions and be sheltered from danger and destruction. So you see, free will is good if we use it to our advantage- and that is to please God.

Another reason why many will be lost is that they are not spiritually awakened. At least not yet. The word of God says that we should ask and it shall be given you; seek and ye shall find... [Luke 11:9]. So many have tapped into the spirit world not to encounter God but the devil and his entities. If individuals sincerely seek God with all their hearts, He will come to them quickly. The rigor and the challenges of life alone should inform us that something is wrong, and the Bible confirms this. The fall of man has taken a toll on the whole earth, including man himself. That's why Jesus came to reconcile man back to God. Man has a second chance of living forever in paradise! How awesome is that? If you do not feel that right now, repent, ask God to forgive you of all the sins you've ever committed, and then invite him into your life. I do not care what may be happening in your life now; God is Greater.

So many people are just merely getting by, knowing not that there are dangers ahead. The Bible emphatically warns us about spiritual blindness. When a person is blind physically, that individual is helpless and vulnerable. However, this kind of blindness is less severe than spiritual blindness. The Bible went as far as to compare this kind of blindness with wickedness!

The way of the wicked is as darkness: They know not at what they stumble.

PROVERBS 4:19

Thus, there is hope for those who are still in the valley. The war is still raging. There are still more faking lions to be conquered.

Moreover, there are still more victims to be delivered and set free. As you read this book, someone is about to give up and throw in the towel. I was on a particular social media platform a while back when I saw this young woman pop up and start telling her story of being plagued by a suicide demon. She said she grew up in a spiritual home and got baptized at a tender age (in her teens) but didn't understand what it takes to serve or to be a child of God. Now, at the age of about 16, this suicide demon that plagued her all the days of her life became more persistent. She was having more frequent attacks than ever before. She would hear voices in her head telling her to kill herself. Then she took off in a car and ran into someone but was unsuccessful.

Then the voice told her to let go of the gas and steering wheel and head straight through a bustling, heavy traffic intersection one day.

During the ordeal, the voice told her to cover her eyes with her hands. As she shot forward and waited for the big explosion, nothing happened. She stated that it was as if she was escorted across the intersection (supernaturally) over to the other side. Then she heard sirens behind her. She bolted out of her car and ran up to the policeman, asking him to kill her. I must say that this must be one of the most aggressive suicide demons anyone has ever come across. The adversary cannot harm, or touch God's chosen without permission. One of the most common weapons of the devil is the manipulation of the mind. He could do considerable damage if he could infiltrate an individual's mind and take complete control.

The mind is the control center of your whole being. Thoughts begin to first process in your mind. The mind is also called the heart or the core of one's very being (spiritually speaking). The Bible tells us to keep our hearts with all diligence, for out of it exudes life issues. [Proverbs 4:23]. The adversary of our souls acknowledges that if we are unable to retain the mind of Christ in us through His word and our obedience, he can quickly attack, tear down, and plunder our city. When the word of God is in us, undoubtedly, it is sharper than any two-edged sword ripping through the enemy's scheme. The devil can't stand the word of God. It comes with too much power and authority! If he tries to use it, it would be in a sarcastic kind of way. [Matthew 4:3]. Do you see how important it is to know the word of God? You cannot conquer life's faking lions without it. Intimidation is one of the devil's weapons against humanity. Goliath's shout was confirmed, as was his armor, spear, shield, and stature, but not his gods. The individual who knows better and moves accordingly has the most advantage.

Now David knew right there that it was a play on the mind. However, he wasn't going to buy it. Why? Because he knew something that Goliath didn't know- and that is a much more significant and mightier warrior who never loses a battle! So, while the Philistine army was in great hype because of their big, strong man and the army of Israel was cowering because of his voice, David was red hot, ready for a showdown. Being anointed as the next king of Israel, David knew that Goliath wouldn't be able to defeat him. Let me pause and ask someone: What is life throwing at you that makes you want to run and cower under some not-so-protective shelter for the rest of your days? Have you ever thought that there is someone much more significant than your problems?

Well, it's time to face the music. God made us to win! If we have been made in the image and likeness of God, then He didn't make an image of defeat. Life will make sense when we gird our loins, pull our bootstraps, and 'quit ye like men and be strong'! Therefore, if we seek God with all our hearts, we will begin to see an undeniable destiny. Critics may say there is no hope for you- some may even write you off. You may feel neglected, rejected, downcast, or even downtrodden; However, that's when Almighty God will rush in and turn your darkness into day. God made us to inherit till he comes. Now He gave us choices: to choose Him and live forever or to reject Him and perish in hell. Thus, if we think we can find real, abundant life outside Him, we are in for a rude awakening. If we stick to His divine plan, we will be significantly rewarded.

It's time to throw all whining out the door and be grateful for everything. God truly deserves our worship and adoration. After all, that's what He made us for. Let us find our true purpose and enjoy it to the fullest. Scriptures declare that man's whole duty is to fear God and keep His commandments. [Ecclesiastes 12:3] When we change our minds (when our minds are renewed in Christ Jesus), we will look at life differently despite our circumstances. Many are asking today, "Does life make any sense?" They looked around, and all they could see were heartaches, pains, and discontentment. Many folks are on the brink of being suicidal. However, there is an answer to life's trials and woes- God Himself. Jesus is the answer for the whole world today. However, He orchestrated it to be so from the beginning of time, and no one can change it. Without Him, all life's living is vain.

Now we see why we face so many difficulties in life- It won't work without Almighty God. Many of us know this truth, but how do we respond? This is where self- destruct kicks in. Despite the awareness that Godlessness leads to destruction, individuals continue to live as if they can make it on their own or if someone else can rescue them. This is a state of delusion. God explicitly states that there is none other besides Him. How is it for humanity, who God made in His image and likeness and with great intelligence, to act like the lowest class of animals? We have deceived ourselves so much for so long that our minds seem irreformable. The harmful lifestyle we learned and adopted from our parents is now passed on to our children. Now, our children pass it on to their children and grandchildren.

Thus, the vicious cycle of harmful living continues. Do not be surprised, my friend; a toxic lifestyle is one without God and filled with sinfulness. There is nothing negative or harmful about God. God is pure Light, and there is no darkness in Him. Negativity is filled with darkness. There is no peace on the negative side of life. A make-believe peace is deceptive, and is of the prince of darkness, and only lasts for a while. This is why an individual would get high on drugs this minute, which causes them to forget about their troubles and woes for a while, and the next minute, they are back in the same or even worse state than before! Until we all understand the true meaning of life, we will always be going around in circles.

It's not God's intention for His beloved ones to wander like lost sheep without a shepherd. When God made man in His image and likeness, it was for Him to have a close relationship with His Creator. The love that God has for humanity would not allow Him to leave man up to destruction despite their fallen state. In this case, He counseled with Himself how He might redeem him:

> *But when the fulness of time come, God sent forth his son, made of a woman, made under the law, to redeem them that were under the law, that we may receive the adoption of sons.*

GALATIANS 4:4-5

Thus, God came as a man to rescue, restore, and deliver him from ultimate destruction. Humanity has a second chance, but will we be willing to submit to His sovereignty and be saved from the pending judgment? Despite not seeing God face to face or hearing him speaking to you directly, it does not necessarily mean He doesn't exist. The breath that we breathe but cannot see confirms the presence of God living inside us. He blew a measure of Himself in us so that we become alive! Now we know what happens when He pulls back what He blew in us. We should be grateful to God for our very existence. Notwithstanding, there is a particular reason why we were created- to worship the Creator.

Nothing will function as it should when a man misses his true purpose in life. Instead, everything will spiral while God waits for man to return to consciousness. Many are waiting to be wealthy, for life to have some form of meaning, while those who are wealthy are still looking for some sense of life by seeking more wealth. However, the Holy Scriptures declare that a man's life does not consist of the abundance of things he possesses. True happiness comes from God. Horatio Gates Spafford, an American lawyer and the pastor of a Presbyterian church, lost everything in the 'Great Chicago Fire' in 1871.

To make matters worse, a few years later, he lost his four daughters at sea on a sea vessel headed to England. Instead of having a nervous breakdown or blaming God for all his woes, Spafford was inspired. He went on to write the famous hymn: "It Is Well With My Soul," also known as "When Peace, Like A River."

Think about having everything life offers; then, it's all gone. What would have been your reaction? Will you bless the Lord like Job did, or would you blaspheme His name and perish? Life is easy and will look great when an individual seems prosperous.

However, if things take a spiral, the individual's attitude will determine whether he comes out more triumphant than ever or not. We will always know what an individual is made up of when he undergoes a certain amount of pressure and emerges victorious. Someone once said, "Life is one big road with many signs." This statement does make a lot of sense. This is because we know that life's road is not just a straight path. Sometimes, we may hit a bend, a curb, or even a few crossroads and dead ends. No wonder we need divine intervention- a compass, and that is, the Word of God:

Thy word is a lamp unto my feet and a light unto my path.

PSALM 119:105

Life will begin to make sense when we surrender all to Jesus Christ of Nazareth. God, who is sovereign over all, knows exactly what is good for us and our souls. Let us not forget that it is Him who made us and not we ourselves. He alone can do exceedingly abundantly above all we can think or imagine. Wouldn't you surrender all to a God like that? When we submit to God, then we will experience his excellent greatness!

O taste and see that the Lord is good: Blessed is the man that trusteth in Him.

PSALM 34: 8

When we add it all up, there is no disappointment in God.

The Samaritan woman didn't know the meaning of life until she met the Messiah. She has been rejected and ostracized by society for being an adulteress. Nevertheless, she encountered the Law Giver, who forgave her of her sinful lifestyle and gave her another chance at righteous living. The Scriptures declare that she ran and left her water pot to tell others about her newfound faith in Jesus Christ, the Messiah. Many of us may be looked down on by families and society at one point- maybe because of our shortcomings. However, how many of us know that God makes the final decision in our lives? We may feel cast down, rejected, ostracized, and neglected, but remember that God has made us and not us, ourselves. Despite what may befall an individual, God still says, "Here I am; repent, surrender all to me, and I'll fix it."

Many people lose hope because they lack faith that God can do anything for them. I must honestly say that that's a sad state to be in. Unbelief is like a poison that goes deep down into the core of one's whole being and causes an intoxication that is incurable! These folks decided that life did not make sense to them. They have been in the clutches of the enemy for so long that their only hope is to make some money, try to get rich, win the lotto or the cash pot drawings, and live a life of splurging before they die. What extravagant wasting of one's soul! The souls of men are so important to God that He came and shed His own blood for us. [Acts 20:28]. Do we see how serious a matter the lives of men are to God? God had was to stop Saul dead in His tracks when He went hunting for the heads of Christians. He could have killed Saul, but he saw something in Saul He could use for His honor and glory.

Saul, a zealot and a Jew of the Mosaic law who grew up at the feet of a master 'rabbi' (teacher) Gamaliel, out of sheer ignorance, decided to persecute the Christians in the name of the Mosaic or Judaic law. Indeed, it wasn't a great idea. Jesus confronted him on the Damascus Road, took his eyesight, and knocked him down senselessly. Instead of destroying this young man, God decided to use him, despite him causing the deaths of so many Christians. Saul's life was changed drastically after one encounter with Jesus Christ the Righteous. Your life can be changed too (if you've not yet accepted Jesus Christ as your LORD and Savoir) by only a look at the crucified one. Then you'll begin to see that life does make sense after all.

We should never think that an individual life can't be changed because of their wicked lifestyle. The word of God declares that we have all sinned and come short of the glory of God. [Romans 3:23] No one has done any good, no not one. Therefore, no one can point a finger at another!

> *Thou meetest him that rejoiceth and worketh righteousness, those that remember thee in thy ways: behold thou art wroth; for we have sinned: in those is continuance, and we shall be saved. But we are all as an unclean thing, and all our righteousness are as filthy rags; And we all do fade as a leaf; and our iniquities, like the wind, have taken us away. And there is none that calleth upon thy name, that stirreth up himself to take hold of thee; for thou hast hid thy face from us, because of our iniquities.*

> ISAIAH 64:5-7

The prophet Isaiah didn't hold back from rebuking the self-righteousness of the people. We live in a very chaotic and reckless society, as this book is being read. Our nations are gone so far from God that our self-righteousness justifies everything that we do. Offenses come quickly; so are the lawsuits, and everyone seems justified in their own way. However, crimes against God's laws and ordinances only increased, and none considered it. The fear of God had fled from man, and therefore, we continue to tread dangerously!

Many who have wasted their time on earth will give an account at the great white throne judgment. To think of it, many had the opportunity to make their life meaningful by considering where they would like to spend their long eternity. Unfortunately, most people are waiting to cross over to the other side of life to find out where they will end up. This, of course, is a very unwise and foolish decision; by then, it will be too late. Instead of accepting Jesus Christ as their LORD and Savior now, they would rather wait and see their fate. There and then, God's mercy would have long passed! Soldiers who are enlisted in an army expect that there will be a war sometime in the future; thus, they will always make the necessary preparations. God sent His word into the world to prepare us for His coming. God, who is sovereign over all, could have communicated with us differently. However, He chose to do so through the patriarchs, prophets, priests, apostles, and the written Word.

To reject God's written Word is to reject Him. There is no excuse on that great day of judgment:

> *Therefore, we ought to give the more earnest heed to the things which we have heard, lest at any time we should let them slip. For if the word spoken by angels was steadfast, and every transgression and disobedience received a just recompense of reward; how shall we escape, If we neglect so great salvation; which at the first began to be spoken by the LORD and was confirmed unto us by them that heard Him; God also bearing them witness, both with signs and wonders, and with divers miracles, and gifts of the Holy Ghost, according to His own will?*

HEBREWS 2:1-4

We can come to one conclusion that our conscience and the intelligence God had bestowed on man will testify against them on that day.

CHAPTER 6
THE SILENT BATTLE RAGES ON

As this world rapidly approaches the end of time, a war rages silently. Inevitably, everyone is either directly or indirectly engaged in this warfare. Many are involved without even knowing it. This is the hour where many embraced evil for good and good for evil. Unfortunately, most people aren't aware that we live in a time of deception. Millions have been deceived by many daily, and they, in turn, deceived many! Oh, what a world we are experiencing today! It is a world of turmoil. This is a spiritual battle we are fighting, and it intensifies every minute of the hour. No one needs a pair of eyeglasses to see what's happening in this world. It is not necessary. Even the beasts of the fields and nature show us that something is happening. Nevertheless, many refused to wake up or even think twice about what they were experiencing.

Painkillers are the order of the day. Some would instead become zombies (If there is ever such a thing) instead of waking up and facing reality. As time flies rapidly away, the numbness becomes deafening. Folks do not even care about their lives anymore. A spirit of self-destructiveness kicks in when a society reaches a certain level or extent where nothing matters anymore. We live in a society where everyone thinks they have the solution for the issues people face. To put more adhesive on the already necrotic site, they trained more individuals (in psychological counseling) who needed healing themselves. We have become a sick society who do not care for the only real and natural remedy for our lives, which is salvation from Jesus Christ of Nazareth, the son of the living God. Yes, there is a war going on, my friend, and the question is, when the smoke is cleared, on which side will you be?

We cannot afford to wait until the battle is over (of a surety, it will be very soon) before we decide. By then, it will just be too late. Be informed that individuals who have accepted Jesus Christ today have already engaged in spiritual warfare. The mere fact that you have accepted Jesus Christ (baptized in Jesus Christ's name and received the gift of the Holy Ghost) is a credential or proof that you've been enlisted. Now that we have been enlisted, we must adhere to specific codes and conducts as soldiers of the cross. On that note, I'll digress a little. Many individuals are delighted and non- reluctant to obey rules and protocols when enlisted in a military entity. They don't care about the harsh and rigid discipline that comes with the package. All they think about is that I am a soldier, and I've made a vow to live or to die for my state or my country, for that matter. On the other hand, they objected to enlisting in God's spiritual and military entity. Some folks must have heard or witnessed God's children endure persecution and long-suffering.

There is no doubt about it: if we avoid fighting for righteousness today, the consequences will come tomorrow. We will never fully understand or even acknowledge that a battle is raging until we come to Christ. When our eyes are lit, we will realize that the battle in the spirit world cannot be fought with natural or ordinary weapons such as bombs, guns, spears, swords, etc. The Bible states that the weapons of our warfare are not carnal but mighty through God... [2 Corinthians 10:4]. So, I recalled this scripture to emphasize that God did not leave us helpless, powerless, or without arsenals. He knew the impact of His words, especially in unity with His spirit! There is no telling the power that also comes with praying and fasting. Put it this way: it's called the SPF (study, pray, and fast) strategy. When contemplating overcoming and being victorious over spiritual conflict, God gave me this insight a while back.

The SPF strategy extension is called the 'Supernatural Power of Fortification"! Whew! Are you ready to rattle Hell's foundation? Then let's do it together! There is still a little time left. I mentioned the earthly army and the soldier ready for battle. Now, the attire of the spiritual soldier is much more unique. We must first know who or what we are fighting against. Seeing that we wrestle not against flesh and blood but principalities and powers, the ruler of darkness of this world and spiritual wickedness in high places, we must put on the whole armor of God. In this case, Salvation becomes our helmet; Faith becomes our shield; the Holy Spirit becomes our sword; righteousness becomes our breastplate; Truth becomes our belt or girding; and the Gospel of Peace becomes our boots. There you have it. We are fully armored. Don't ever leave home without your armor! To face any battle, an individual should always be prepared. Many of us have fallen multiple times in this spiritual battle in which we have been engaged. This is because we were ignorant of the battleground (which first starts in mind) and the strategy of fighting, so instead, we wandered around and became prey to the onslaught of the enemy.

The adversary seems to be roaring, but is he a lion? If you are ignorant of the spirit world, you would think this is some excellent, uncontrollable monster unleashed on humanity. Don't be deceived; the devil has power, but that is restricted. The Devil can't do anything unless God allows him to. Jesus told his disciples as he was about to ascend that all power is given unto him in heaven and earth. [Matthew 28:18]. So now, looking back at these scriptures, we can only come to one conclusion, and that is that Jesus is the Boss.

Another scripture also attests to this: at the name of Jesus, every knee shall bow in heaven and earth, and every tongue should confess that Jesus Christ is Lord to the glory of God the Father. Thus, knowing these things, we should not give the enemy any form of credit or reverence because he is not God Almighty.

When an individual has little to no knowledge of the spirit world, he becomes like a ship tossed to and fro with every kind of deception and crude manipulation of the prince of darkness- Satan, the old dragon. This individual may get up in the morning, do their morning routine, such as wash their face, brush their teeth, have some breakfast, get dressed, and head out to their work or whatever their plan is for the day and doesn't even have the slightest clue that the enemy is there just waiting for an opportunity to destroy them. Sadly, many who encounter this book will forget most of what is written, which is perfectly fine. What is more critical is that we never forget the things written in the holy scriptures. All the things that are written in the Bible will indeed be fulfilled. Why? Because God divinely inspires them. If God promises us that the head of the serpent is going to be crushed, then it's going to be crushed. Whether you choose to believe or not, God's decision still stands.

In this present time, we are living, the adversary is once again offering the world to as many individuals as possible via blood sacrifice and evil altars. Many have already bitten the bullet. Eventually, many of these individuals realized it wasn't worth it. Daily, they would wear fake smiles but, deep down, have a false sense of security. Deep down within, their souls are tormented, and they are slowly dying. Thus, it brought us to the Holy Scriptures:

What does it profit a man to gain the whole world and lose his soul.

MATTHEW 16:26, MARK 8:36

Many individuals are walking around, appearing fine, but their souls cry desperately. Hell has opened her mouth wider than ever, and her fangs are ready to devour! However, Jesus Christ promised His disciples that He would build His church upon the rock and that the gates of hell would not prevail against it. [Matthew 16:18]. It's time to pray! It's time to fast, my friend! It's to hide the word in our hearts so we can stand against the wiles of the Devil. The spiritual fight is on- the war is raging! One old prophet suggested,

Beat your plowshares into swords, and your pruning hooks into spears: let the weak say, I am strong.

It's no time to be frolicking- the enemy plans to kill, steal, and destroy. Yes, my friend, if we think this is false, let's look around for a while. Check your news (the ones that seem authentic) channel or media and see what the order of the day is. The world is presently like a sack overfilled with its content and ready to burst asunder. The signs around us are screaming while the Earth is groaning under pressure. The signs are everywhere! More homeless and hopeless individuals are roaming the streets more than ever. Hopeless people (from every walk of life) seem to be buzzing everywhere! The invisible force of darkness has held these individuals in chains for decades- year in and year out. Blinded by the inability to discern the spiritual world, they continue in chains of misery and hopelessness.

Now, friend, are you ready to be enlisted into the army of God? There is a lot of work to do in the kingdom. Will you roll your sleeves up and be a part of the solution? Jesus told His disciples when he was on earth:

> *But when he saw the multitudes, he was moved with compassion on them, because they fainted, and were scattered abroad, as sheep having no shepherd. Then saith He unto His disciples, the harvest truly is plenteous, but the labourers are few; Pray ye therefore the Lord of the harvest, that he will send forth labourers into the harvest.*

MATTHEW 9:36-38

Many people presently are clueless about their future and destiny. They are lost souls looking for a compass- a sense of direction. Some of us have been in that kind of predicament before but thank God for sending rescue just in time! If it wasn't for His grace and mercies, the enemy would have probably taken us out already, and our souls would have been lost. Think about the many individuals we grew up with, attended school together, etc. A number of these individuals probably lost their lives (maybe through tragic or even natural death) and gone without the blessed hope of eternal life. Spiritual darkness is a deadly poison that is constantly eating away at the souls of humanity. The sooner an individual can escape the prison walls of spiritual darkness, the better.

Some are already aware that they are in this imprisonment of chains and darkness but are hardly making any effort to escape. Sometimes, these poor souls are heavily bound by spiritual shackles. These are also called 'strongholds.' In a spiritual sense, a stronghold is something or someone that securely holds something or someone firmly in place. In other words, it's to place a firm and strong grip on something or someone. This is what the adversary did when He influenced man to sin against God. Because of the disobedience, sin entered, and the Devil used this as a conduit to try and control the lives of humans. Sin belongs to the devil and his angels. He was the original transgressor introducing this lid covered platter of worms to humanity. Undoubtedly, it was the greatest deception of all, and humans have been plagued with anxieties and fears ever since. The result is strongholds that seem to imprison the human soul.

However, the Lamb of God stepped between the destruction and the continual bleeding of the soul and made an atonement for our sins. God's infinite love for us refused to see humanity being destroyed by the wicked plot of the enemy. Man was innocent until he was tempted and fell into sin. God, in His infinite wisdom, knew how He would deal with the situation from the beginning. The enemy's plan had backfired! He was waiting to see how God would have handled the situation. He swore that God would have done it unjustly, but he was in for a rude awakening. Instead of condemning and destroying man, God merely punished them (along with the serpent) and gave them a promise at the same! The devil thought he would have won man over unto his side, but it didn't work!

And I will put enmity between thee and the woman, and between thy seed and her seed; it shall bruise thy head, and thou shalt bruise his heel.

GENESIS 3: 15

Moreover, God, our Father, had prepared the Lamb slain from the foundation of the world to redeem man from his fallen state. This tells us that the only potentate, Omniscient (all-knowing), Omnipresent (present everywhere), Omnipotent (all- powerful) God knew this event would have taken place before the beginning of time! Now, can we think of something that God doesn't know? Yes, we can! God doesn't know any other God besides Him. [Isaiah 44:8]. Having all this knowledge of God, my friend, we should not be fearful or worried about what is presently happening around us. The wicked enemy of our souls seems to turn the whole world into confusion and chaos, but we don't have to be moved by his evil scheme. Jesus calms the rough, stormy, and choppy sea, and so He is doing the same to situations that are trying to engulf us; "Peace Be Still," Saith the LORD.

The most important thing to know in this life is that the battle that we are facing now is already won. The Director has already written the script and decides how it will end. Now, if we already knew how the end will be by reading the whole plot (the Bible), why are we dismayed by what is happening in this part of the script? Wasn't this supposed to be a part of the whole plot? We must be conscious that the battle will be hard before it improves. It's also important to know which side of the fight you are on. This battle is like none other. This is a very predictable spiritual battle- that is, there is no guessing who will win. That said, we must decide which side we will choose. If we choose the LORD side, we have nothing to fear; the battle is already won, and we are just role players. However, our souls will be secured, and we will eventually live with God in His kingdom forever.

To be lost or miss out on eternal life is a tremendous blow to the unbeliever. There is no more solution for the soul who died without the blessed hope. The Holy Scriptures are always there to encourage us:

Seek ye LORD while He may be found, called upon Him while He is near: let the wicked forsake his way, and the unrighteous man his thoughts: and let him return unto the LORD, and he will have mercy upon him; and to our God, for He will abundantly pardon.

ISAIAH 55:6

After going through hell and high water here on Earth, wouldn't it be great to know that we have hope that makes us not ashamed? The same promise that fell on Abraham is that we can inherit over on the other side of this Jordan if we are only faithful. Jesus told His disciples that He had prepared a mansion for all who wait for Him. God is always faithful to His promise, and none He has spoken will fail.

Individuals are walking around, carrying their loads or burdens, fighting their battles, and failing miserably because they refuse to allow the Light of Christ to shine into their hearts. Often, their trust is only in man and the things they see around them. They have no clue that they are under a curse. God spoke through His prophet Jeremiah to tell His people that the man who trusts in a man is cursed:

Thus, saith the LORD; Cursed be the man that trusteth in man, and maketh flesh his arm, and whose heart departeth from the LORD. For he shall be like the heath in the desert, and shall not see when good cometh; but shall inhabit the parched places in the wilderness, in a salt land and not inhabited.

JEREMIAH 17: 5-6

There are many benefits to serving the LORD.

However, individuals should not come to Christ simply because of the benefits. As Christ has laid His life down for us, we should be willing to do the same. In other words, the love in Christ should be found in us so that we won't be hesitant to surrender everything to Him.

When we follow suit, this love will quickly transfer to those around us who are hurting and need to be rescued, restored, and delivered. Often, unbelievers find themselves under pressure and can't even explain or understand why. A vigilant child of God would immediately detect that it's an attack from hell, but what or how should an unbeliever respond? To fight and overcome these dark entities, one must first analyze and evaluate the impact of the assault. Although Some attacks may seem frivolous (intent merely to distract), we as children of God should take every attack seriously. At the same time, we must stay calm and collected. The enemy is determined to prevent us from experiencing the luxury that he had lost and would do everything in his power to stop us from inheriting this legacy that Jesus had promised.

What time is it? It's time to fight! The last time I checked, the people who were baptized in Jesus's name and bear the Holy Ghost (the spiritual 'Ark of the Covenant') were called to be soldiers of the cross. In other words, we are warriors- and when the battle is hot, warriors have no time to rest! One songwriter declares, 'Fight be brave against all evil…never run or even lay behind…If you'll win for God and the Right, keep on the firing line.'

There is no doubt that the fight is on. As I write this book, somebody is fighting a suicide spirit right now. Someone may be contemplating a homicide or a rape assault, or even a robbery. All these circumstances stem from demonic oppression and influences. An individual can be triggered at any given time if there is a demonic stronghold in their life. These adverse circumstances are demonic activities trying to cause chaos and destruction. Some may be skeptical of this truth, but a spiritual person would gladly approve. This is because there is zero spiritual insight without a covenant or an altar. On this note, I must stress that you can receive nothing from the spirit world if you are not involved. This involvement must always be positive or godly, for that matter. Some folks are involved in the spirit world without even being aware! That is scary. Warning! Being in covenant with demons and devils is self-destructive!

Humans must interact with two worlds- the physical or natural world we are accustomed to and the spiritual one. Now, the spiritual world is even more active than the physical. Thus, what's in the physical world results from the spiritual. Are we going somewhere now? This is why our lives become more complex: the spiritual world always brings new stuff, ideas, and creativity into the physical world. We receive all these luxuries because they were there before in the spiritual world. Now, back to the spiritual things of the spiritual world. These can either be positive or negative.

First, an altar must be erected for a portal to be created. This portal will allow access in and out of the spirit world. As I warned before, to raise an altar, one must first acknowledge for whom the altar was raised. This is because an altar is a place where sacrifice is made.

> *And the LORD appeared unto Abram, and said, Unto thy seed will I give this land: and there builded he an altar unto the LORD who appeared unto him. And he removed from thence unto a mountain on the east Bethel, and pitch his tent, having Bethel on the west and Hai on the east: and there he builded on altar unto the LORD, and call upon the name of the LORD.*

> GENESIS 12:7-8

So, we see that an altar was made to offer sacrifice to Almighty God. Now, where there is an altar, there is a portal. As long as God's people initiate an altar, they can access the throne. Fleeing from his brother Esau, Jacob encountered God at the place where his grandfather Abraham raised an altar some decades ago:

> *And Jacob went from Beersheba, and went toward Haran. And he lighted upon a certain place, and tarried there all night because the sun was set; and he took of the stones of that place, and put them for pillows, and lay down in that place to sleep. And he dreamed, and behold a ladder set up on the earth, and the top of it reached to heaven: and behold the angels of God ascending and descending on it. And, behold the LORD stood above it, and said, I am the LORD God of Abraham thy father, and the God of Isaac: the land whereon thou liest, to thee will I give it and to thy seed; and thy seed shall be as the dust of the earth and thou shalt spread abroad to the west, and*

to the east, and to the north, and to the south: and in thee and in thy seed shall all the families of the earth be blessed.

And And behold I am with thee and will keep thee in all places whither thou goest, and will bring thee again into this land; for I will not leave thee until I have done that which I have spoken to thee of. And Jacob waked out of his sleep and said, how dreadful is this place! This is none other but the house of God, and this is the gate of heaven. And Jacob rose up early in the morning, and took the stone that he had put for his pillows, and set it up for a pillar, and poured oil upon the top of it. And he called the name of that place Bethel: but the name of that city was called Luz at the first.

GENESIS 28:10-18

This passage of Scripture alone has so many deep, obscure, and powerful insights that it will blow your mind. However, let's move on to our primary focus. So, this tells us that it doesn't matter how long the altar was there. As long as it is being initiated, it's a covenant that opens a portal to the spiritual world! Now, the point I am making is that there are two altars to the spirit world- the altar unto God and an evil altar unto the prince of Darkness. As I warned before, sacrificing on an evil altar will lead to self- destruction. The Devil intends to captivate the soul of an individual. Covenanting with an evil altar is the last thing a person would want to do. It is opening Hell to you, your family, friends, and folks affiliated with you.

This is where the problem arose: ungodly folks sacrificing on evil altars and giving unclean spirits access to the lives of other persons. These unclean spirits are poised to cause chaos and destruction in individual lives. Thus, the battle rages on, but it is ever so silent because many are ignorant of the cause and effect of circumstances in their lives and the lives of others.

CHAPTER 7
EVIDENCE OF TWO UNSEEN FORCES

Undoubtedly, most of us can attest that two opposing forces exist. One is the Force of light (which represents righteousness, goodness, and purity), and the other is the force of darkness, which means everything evil, unjust, impure, and destructive. If you haven't yet come to grips with this fact, you may not be living in this world. The truth is that we see these two forces operating in and around us all the days of our lives. Remember that these two forces are at work as you read this book. Jesus declares to his disciples that He is the Light of the world. In Him, Jesus, there is no darkness at all.

However, He also informed His disciples that the prince of darkness (Satan, also called the ruler of darkness of this world) is on an assignment: to kill, steal, and destroy. Do you see the big picture now? We, as human beings, are caught in a tug of war!

As we exist in this world, it's almost impossible for anyone not to be influenced by either of these two entities. It doesn't matter who you are: religious or not, atheist or not, righteous or not, good or not, whatever category you are identified with; you have been influenced by either of these entities. Now, some laws and consequences come with affiliation with either force. There is unspeakable righteousness, peace, and joy with the force of Light (Jesus Christ himself). Not only does one receive the complete heavenly package, but that individual will never be the same. The outstanding work of salvation is so strong, powerful, and profound that it still causes many to wonder (particularly an unsaved individual) when they encounter a Holy Ghost-filled believer whom God has snatched from the kingdom of darkness and transformed into a son of God!

I heard it before. One preacher suggested that greatness can't be seen, but its presence can be felt. How true. How often have you been to a gathering, for example, an event where great people or so-called great names were present? Even if you had some accolades under your belt, how did you feel? Oh, maybe that venue was too local; let's look at the real side of greatness. How about a place, a sanctuary (not any ordinary sanctuary) where the power of God is bursting out sporadically like little flames of fire? Have you ever experienced anything of the sort? Well, I can attest to that, that I have. I have gone to sanctuaries where the glory of Almighty God was so rich that it confirmed that of a truth where His presence is; his kingdom is there also! [Luke 17:20]. I have experienced the power and glory of Almighty God many times since I have been saved. However, two significant encounters will stick with me forever. I won't recall them now, but I will leave them for upcoming chapters.

The body of a human being is like a house that the soul inhabits. Your soul is the real you. He operates through and relies on the five senses (the eyes to see, the ear ears, the hands to feel or touch, the mouth to taste or eat, and finally, the nose to smell) to enhance his intelligence of this world. Thus, if all these body systems become defective due to different circumstances in life, such as an accident, old age, lousy management, etc., the soul is almost ready to depart. Now, these senses can be used by the soul or the mind to make decisions or make sound judgments. One sense that has an instant connection to the spirit world is the sense of feeling. In this sense, it is like knowing immediately when the climate changes! That feeling of either being hot, lukewarm, or cold.

Thus, the word of God prompts us not to make decisions according to how we feel. Our feelings heavily rely on or depend on our emotions, which are highly triggered by our mind, which is the master control of our total being. With, let us go deeper into the vault. When an individual opens his mind and spirit to absorb the spiritual things of Almighty God, a shaking suddenly occurs and goes deep down into the core of their being. That's God Himself! It's like a vast individual trying to fit into a little house. This is called surrendering to God, the only authentic, potentate, and sovereign being- Jesus Christ, our Righteousness. Don't get it twisted; I know what you may be thinking. Doesn't the devil agent operate in the same way? Yes, they do. The adversary is a big-time copycat and a mimicking menace! As we all may be aware, Jesus came as the Christ (the Anointed One), He the devil came as the antichrist (the opposer or the enemy of the Christ), and God executes his work through three offices, the Father, the Son and the Holy Spirit; The devil works through the offices of the antichrist, the false prophets, and false preachers and teachers.

So, then, we see that the main motive of the devil is to deceive as many individuals as possible. For example, if an individual isn't seriously seeking after God and just playing around, then that individual may eventually find themselves in the wrong assembly. Yes, Satan has his gathering also, and if a person has no spiritual discernment, then they will be worshipping the devil without even knowing it! Does that sound very eerie? Indeed! Without spiritual eyesight, the road may look enticing and beautiful until one reaches the end of it. Then, we will see that it was a 'dead end' or even a precipice.

Sometimes, the individual has gone so far that it almost seems impossible to return. This is when the enemy seems to drain every strength from the core of your being, and everything around you say it is no use trying to go back; it's over.

This unseen force of darkness will overwhelm an individual, and if God Almighty doesn't step in and push back the enemy, then destruction is inevitable. We can see this force active in drug addiction; we can see this force active in sexual promiscuity and pornography, and the whole nine yards. Some may think these activities are merely choices that some people choose to make, but one must think carefully when this kind of circumstance hits home. Oh yes, I mean when it becomes personal. When one of your loved ones finds him or herself in this kind of predicament, then there will be a wake- up call that something else is happening. There is a wicked force behind these activities. Unfortunately, many will ignore this fact and move along as if it's just a part of life. So let us reason now since you got so far reading this book. If these circumstances are just a part of life, then we could assume that nobody on this face of the earth is immune to them, right? So how is it that you (Let us think that you are in a total sobriety state of being) and I are not victims? Is it because of our skillfulness in riding the tides of life? Or because we are just fortunate? I may surprise you by saying it is none of the above!

You see, the thing with these two unseen forces is that the One (which is the Light of man) is vehemently trying to bring us, as God-made-man, back to sanity while the opposing force (which is the force of darkness) intended for us to go stalk staring mad. Now, this brought me to the point that I want to make: if there were only one or no unseen forces at all, wouldn't you think that everyone and everything existing on this earth right now would agree with each other? Now, let's venture deep into the woods. If there are no unseen forces, how did you and I come into existence? Let me digress a little, seeing that your cerebrum is sparking. Now, we can rule out 'the Big Bang theory' reasoning because the law of nature, which is of superintelligence, tells us that everything (how the earth and everything in it were made) was done in uniformity and order. In other words, for example, plants and trees grow upright, not upside down. Animals walk on their legs, not on their backs or their heads! Insects crawl on their belly, not their backs; you got the picture.

Now, here is the thing: we are assuming that there are no unseen forces for reasoning. Let us ask the question then: are we self-existent? And if so, be the case, how is it that we can't preserve our lives or the lives of our loved ones (who passed away) and their state of being? How long can an individual go without sleeping and not having a nervous breakdown? The truth is that when we start to look into these factors with the innate intelligence ingrained into every human being from conception, we can only come to one conclusion: that there is a supernatural intelligent being and master of the universe that filled all things. Mark, well, I said there is one who makes and controls everything. Everything else, including the force of darkness, is subordinate to Him.

As you can see, I didn't even use any Holy Scriptures from the Bible to make my point. In other words, even if you are ignorant of the word of God, I would assume that sobriety or consciousness should be kicking at your intelligence and that there is an unseen force to be reckoned with. Now you can see that without this force fighting for us men (whom He made in His image and likeness), we would all be destroyed by the opposing force of darkness. This led us to what I mentioned earlier. It would just not be some, but all of us would probably be on drugs, gross sexual immorality, and all manner of wickedness. Believe it or not, all these negative traits are from the prince of darkness. Thus, we have work to do, which is aligning ourselves with the force of Light so we can assist in pushing back this wicked and opposing force of darkness.

Whether an individual wishes to embrace this fact or not, the evidence is undeniable. The two forces that influence humanity are Light and Darkness. Another way to describe the same is Good and Evil. God is all light, and there is no darkness in Him. However, the Devil (Also called the accuser of the brethren) is known as the Prince of Darkness. This tells us that he is an opposer, and he plans to steal, kill, and destroy. The Devil is also seen as a deceiver, and there is no good or righteousness in him. A simple-minded individual who is ignorant of the Devil and his devices would soon fall prey. Thus, Jesus would have to come as the Messiah to rescue us from the onslaught of the Wicked one. Now, when we immerse in water (in the name of Jesus) and are filled with the Holy Ghost, we can stand against the enemy's attack.

During the era of the apostles, Jesus promised to send help (the Comforter) to His people so that they may be able to conquer and destroy the works of darkness:

But ye shall receive power, after that the Holy Ghost comes upon you: and ye shall be witnesses unto me both in Jerusalem and in all Judea. And in Samaria, and unto the uttermost part of the earth.

ACTS 1: 8

Engaging in spiritual warfare without the proper weaponry could be catastrophic. Too many people claim to be Christians and have no enemy engagements because they are clueless about the art of spiritual warfare. Often, I suggested that there are specific criteria a person must possess to be called a Christian. An Israelite is identified by the bloodline they were born of or born into- that is, the bloodline of their forefathers, Abraham, Isaac, and Jacob. The term Christian has been dragged in the muck for too long! Nevertheless, the folks back then in Antioch knew precisely what they were saying when they coined this name on the disciples.

The disciples were called Christians because of their mighty works and the signs that followed them. In other words, their actions and the same result remind the folks of Jesus Christ of Nazareth, who went about healing the sick, raising the dead, casting out demons, etc. Now, when they see these signs and wonders, they are told that these men are followers of Christ. To be a follower of Christ, we must be born into the kingdom- Born of the water, the spirit, and the blood! Eventually, not only will we become followers of Christ, but we will also become sons of God! God now sees us as His children! This is because of the New Birth. Without the New Birth, we would only deceive ourselves.

Something is bound to take place when we follow the instructions given to the apostles. It's a supernatural and divine intervention that starts a change on the inside and burns outwardly! Thus, we have a New Birth experience:

Therefore if any man be in Christ, he is a new creature: old things are passed away; behold, all things are become new.

2 CORINTHIANS 5:17

Now that we are new creatures (citizens of the kingdom of God), we can do things that we have never done before with the empowerment of the Holy Ghost within us. The Holy Ghost enables us to lay hands on the sick, pray for them (that they may be healed), raise the dead, bind and cast demons out of the possessed, and pull down and destroy strongholds.

To tap into the spiritual realm, an individual must be in sync with the Holy Ghost and be backed by faith. God is a Spirit, and there are protocols for accessing His presence. Moreover, He is Holy, which means we must agree with His words and what He requires of us to achieve positive results. When the High Priest goes into the Most Holy Place (to offer sin offerings to God), he must dress, act, and move in a certain way. Moreover, he must be holy-that is, no sin should be found in him, lest he die in the presence of the Lord:

> *And the LORD said unto Moses, Speak unto Aaron, thy brother, that he come not at all times into the holy place within the vail before the mercy seat, which is upon the ark; that he die not: for I will appear in the cloud upon the mercy seat. Thus shall Aaron come into the holy place: with a young bullock for a sin offering and a ram for a burnt offering. He shall put on the holy linen coat, and he shall have the linen breeches upon his flesh, and shall be girded with a linen girdle, and with the linen mitre shall he be attired: these are holy garments; Therefore shall he wash his flesh in water, and so put them on.*

LEVITICUS 16: 2-4

God is a God of uniformity; thus, everything should be done decently and in order. This also depicts the infinite intelligence of God.

> *For precept must be upon precept, precept upon precept; line upon line; here a little, and there a little.*

ISAIAH 28:10

Even though our God tends to be invisible, He had made Himself known to the children of Israel in times past, and today, he has revealed Himself through the person of Jesus Christ of Nazareth. He had spoken to the prophets of old centuries ago regarding His way of entry into the world.

> *For unto us a child is born, unto us a son is given: and the government shall be upon His shoulder: and His name shall be called Wonderful, Counsellor, The mighty God, The everlasting Father, The Prince of Peace.*

> ISAIAH 9:6

Despite God making Himself known to humanity through Jesus Christ, many still didn't receive Him. Some even went to the extent of disapproving of His way of entry into the world. We have no power to choose how God manifests Himself to us or the world, for that matter. He is obligated to no one. Whether we believe in Him or not, it's up to us. However, there is a consequence for unbelief. Most people quickly believe a lie even when there is concrete evidence of irrationalism. Jesus didn't have to come to prove to us that there is a God- The heavens already declared Him to us and every magnificent thing that existed. The issue was for us to know Him (intimately) and what He requires of us.

Merely acknowledging that God exists wouldn't cut it. His desire wasn't for us to be like the animals of the fields with little or limited intelligence. Therefore, God created man in His image and gave him dominion over all living things. The Spirit of God formed man from the dust and fashioned him like unto His image. Humans were made to have sweet fellowship with their Creator. We were wonderfully and fearfully made to shew forth the glory of God. If we are not convinced that there is an invisible world with two opposing forces- good and evil- our virtual reality will become real sooner or later! Self-deception is the equivalent of self-destruction. The body is the vessel that houses the soul or the inner man. We know when the body is defective because our inner man first felt it and knows something went wrong. If the body is experiencing any pain or discomfort, the inner man finds and detects what part of the body is having an issue.

Our outward appearance—features, beliefs, expressions, and appearance—reflects our inner man's state. This is why individuals find it difficult to hide their true feelings, no matter how hard they try. Don't be deceived: our true self cannot be seen with the naked eye! Thus, we are all spiritual beings, but many have not yet woken up to this fact. Our minds are the master control of our entire being. When all is said and done, and the smoke is cleared, our inward man, our true self, will be left standing.

Undoubtedly, God orchestrated this so that humans would be given an immortal body that would enable them to live with Him forever.

CHAPTER 8
SPIRITUAL ARMOR AND WARFARE

Being alive and occupied reading this book as a believer (baptized in Jesus' name and filled with the Holy Ghost) is a great blessing. However, reading this book as an unbeliever is an even greater blessing. For this matter, I am pleased to inform you of one thing: whether you believe it or not, you've inadvertently entered a spiritual battleground without even being aware of it. Even since the day you were born! Congratulations! Welcome to the battlefield! There are only two sides; your fate depends on whichever you choose. Oh, I must confess that I didn't know this until I was converted almost three decades ago. You may ask how I reached this conclusion, but I will say this: A secret or a mystery cannot be revealed unless there is a true heart and an intense desire to seek out the same.

In the vast expanse of human experience and encounters, a realm transcends the physical, a battlefield where two opposing entities war against each other- The force of Light against the force of Darkness. Many are at stake, and the result is eternity; humans play a vital role in this warfare. There is no going back now, at least not to the womb (the birthplace and origin of the dust), but towards the Master of Creation- the mover and shaker of everything ever being created. Now, as we delve into the core of this mystical battleground, we will unravel how a child of God equips and adjusts themselves for spiritual combat.

For a devout child of God, the initial steps into spiritual warfare begin with the recognition of their identity as soldiers of the cross and their denial to serve themselves, the flesh, and worldly accreditations. Firstly, the individual must acknowledge that this warfare entails certain kinds of extraordinary weaponization. This war is not fought with earthly weapons, such as guns, knives, swords, bombs, etc. The word of God declares that the weapons of our warfare are not carnal but mighty through God to the pulling down of strongholds. "What does that mean?" Someone might ask. It simply means that what the warriors of God are fighting with cannot be seen with the naked eye! The weapons of our warfare are simplistic and have no form of extravagance. The Bible also declares that we should put on the whole armor of God, which is the total package of our weaponization. This includes the Helmet of Salvation, the Shield of Faith, the Sword of the Spirit, the Breastplate of Righteous, our Loins girt with Truth, and our Feet shod with the preparation of the gospel of Peace. It's extraordinary indeed. But before you become hesitant, I must inform you about the power behind the weaponry.

The way a Christian fight may seem absurd to many who lack spiritual authority, convictions, and deep spiritual insight. This is because of the deception of who the enemy is! God, the Creator and Father of all humanity wasn't meant for man to fight against each other in the first place. Yes, there are some instances where God used His people, Israel, to destroy wicked and rebellious nations to establish His righteousness throughout the earth. However, when Cain murdered his brother Able, God was greatly displeased. He takes it personally when a man kills or murders another, except for the justification of His law (in the Old Testament) given down to humanity. Now, let us find the culprit and the leading cause behind all these animosities and discontents.

In the book of Genesis, chapter 1, the Bible states that after God created all things, He formed man out of the dust and blew the breath of life in him. Afterward, He put the man to sleep (He performed the first anesthesia), took a rib from the man, and made him a woman, who became his wife. Now, the man and his wife were placed in the garden to care for the same. However, they were not alone. Lucifer, also known as Satan, was cast down to the earth with a third of his colleagues. The Bible didn't say when this occurred, but we knew God stopped this rebellion by casting out the evildoers. Thus, with great jealousy, envy, and dissatisfaction, the devil decided to try and destroy man whom God made in His Image and likeness. He went on to persuade Eve (in plucking the fruit from the tree of the knowledge of good and evil) by speaking to her through the mouth of a serpent. Now you know the story well: man transgressed because of disobedience, so sin infiltrated the lives of man and caused an impact or a domino effect that trickled down from generation to generation.

This continued right up to the point of Jesus' entry into the earthly realm. Jesus came to uncover the enemy's dirty deeds and expose his motives. Jesus told His disciples that the devil came to kill, to steal, and to destroy. Humans were somewhat comfortable in their lifestyle until Jesus showed up. This is the reason why it is so hard to win some individuals over. The enemy has so deeply embedded the seed of wickedness that the whole structure surrounding the root has to be broken down to extract that which was planted. That's precisely what Jesus came to do. No wonder the psalmist suggested that a broken and contrite heart God will not despise. He knew that something and someone had to be broken for us to be saved! Hallelujah!

So, when Jesus was broken (The sharp nails pierced through his flesh, hands, and feet) on the cross, everything else was broken except His bones! His loved ones, families, and friends' hearts were broken. When Jesus gave up the ghost, the earth rent, the veil in the temple was broken, and the chains of sin were shattered. Now, this opens a different kind of warfare for the children of God. The enemy was very subtle in disguising himself up to this point. He successfully held all humans in the bondage of sin up to the minute. When Jesus was resurrected, the curse was broken, and the power transfer was completed. The disciples were endowed with supernatural power from on high.

Now, this power given to man by God was not given to man to sit on but to fight that which we weren't able to fight before- and that is the devil and his demons. Long before His passion on the cross, he sent them out as a witness to preach, heal, rescue, and deliver many from demonic oppression and bondage.

When they returned to Him, they said, "Lord, even the devils are subject unto us through thy name." Jesus replied, "I beheld Satan as lightning fall from heaven. Behold, I give unto you the power to tread on serpents and scorpions, and over all the power of the enemy…"

LUKE 10: 17-19

So, we see that the power was initiated even before He went to the cross. How awesome is that! Nevertheless, Jesus told them not to get caught up in the power but to focus more on their name being written in heaven. [Luke 10:20].

To defeat the enemy through the power of Almighty God, we must live at a certain standard in Christ. We can't just get up and decide to cast out devils without consecration and sanctification. We are ready for war when we are fully prepared by building ourselves up spiritually. We all know what happens when an individual enters a conflict without proper preparation. The result will be defeat.

So now, as the children of God go out to battle, they adorn themselves with faith, which is the unwavering belief in the power and providence of almighty God. This faith is the foundation upon which all other spiritual armor is built. This armor (the shield of faith) infused the soul with courage and resilience in the face of adversity. Now righteousness (which is known as the spiritual breastplate) is a moral compass that guides their actions and intentions. Through acts of compassion, integrity, and virtue, they fortify their spiritual defenses, rendering themselves impervious to the assault of the forces of darkness.

Yet, righteousness alone is not enough to withstand the onslaught of the enemy. The spirit must complement it, the sharp sword that cuts through the veils of deception and exposes the plot of the adversary. No lies of the enemy can defeat the truth. In the book of John [John 1: 14], John declares that Jesus was full of 'grace and truth.' Even Jesus himself declares,

I am the way, the truth, and the life…

JOHN 14:6

When you find the truth, it serves as a girdle for the loins that keep your whole armor intact. Without truth, there will be no understanding of why or how to fight. One would be exposed to the onslaught of the enemy without their spiritual helmet. The adversary would have immediately noticed that there was no helmet and, therefore, launched an assault on the head. The helmet signifies salvation, which means you are free through Jesus Christ's blood and, thus, have the authority to execute in this capacity. How unique is this whole armor of God? The entire armor signifies war, yet still, our feet are shod with the preparation of the gospel of peace! Simply put, the armor is all about liberation for all humanity, but to the enemy of our souls, it signifies war. Whew! What kind of armor is this?!

As the battle rages against God's people, may we all find strength and courage, knowing that we are not alone. This is because, amid spiritual warfare, the Lord our God is our ever-present ally and ultimate source of victory. Unlike an earthly army, our battlefield is the world itself. This means that there is no time off for a warrior in Christ! Children of God cannot afford to let down their guard, even though, at times, we become careless- if we are to be honest. Thus, God's grace and mercy always bring us back to sync with Him and His word.

We should show no sign of flinching as we fight the good fight of faith. It's no retreat, no surrender! We should not waver or be wimpy in our decisions to stand up for Jesus Christ. Let us march on with a conquering tread. We may have some little wounds and bruises here and there, but these would only fuel the fire of our determination to push ahead through the Holy Spirit that resides in us. We can never do this by ourselves. It would be a complete failure if we try to make it on our own. Zechariah, a young man born into captivity and of Hebrew descent, was called to be a prophet. Now, God visited Zechariah and showed him things of the past, present, and future regarding the fate of His people, Israel. God told Zechariah to tell His servant Zerubbabel, governor of Judah at that point in time, that the task God was about to wrought through him was not going to be done by might or power:

> Then he answered and spake unto me, saying, this is the word of the LORD unto Zerubbabel, saying, Not by might, nor by power, but by my Spirit, saith the LORD of hosts.

ZECHARIAH 4:6

As children of God, we often wonder how we would maneuver a specific task when given to us by Him. However, God will be the only one shining at the end of the day. He will not give His glory to another, nor will He share it either. This is why He orchestrates this kind of warfare for His children. However, we should not take the arsenals that God handed us lightly. Not because we do not wrestle with flesh and blood means they are ineffective. God's aim is not to destroy humanity or for us to use these arsenals on each other. The ultimate target of these weaponry is the devil and his agents.

There is one common enemy that is trying to destroy all of humanity, and it's the Devil, called Satan, the old Dragon. If we find ourselves fighting against each other, then we will all fail miserably. We will do precisely what the enemy desperately intended- to divide and conquer. If this warfare we are fighting is against flesh and blood, we would have given weaponry to destroy the same. However, God has given us spiritual weapons that are far greater and more effective. Though we can't see it with our natural eyes, the damage to the kingdom of darkness can be devastating. For example, many individuals underestimate the weapon of prayer, but prayer, when done correctly, can be traumatizing to the enemy.

I experienced the power of prayer while working in a particular community as a security officer one night. I used to pray 'on the go' spontaneously, especially just before and after taking my break in a parking lot near the clubhouse. I went to my vehicle just after midnight, and no sooner as I began to pray than I heard demonic voices screaming as they fell from the skies! It was pretty weird, and I was a bit puzzled, for it was the first time I had ever experienced anything like it. To Think about it, I didn't even tell anyone about this; I started remembering these things as I wrote this book. God would have me remember this so individual may know the power of an effectual fervent prayer.

Again, the whole saga of spiritual warfare is not about us but is about Him who called, sent, and charged us to wage war against the enemy of our souls. The battle is raging, even though many can't see. Dual citizenship is required. When you become a citizen of the kingdom of God, you will have access to the spirit realm. This is where events happen spiritually before they are fulfilled physically. You will see things other folks can't- even before they manifest! That's why a true prophet can foretell something before it happens. It's not by might nor power but by the Spirit of the living God. However, some individuals have signed up and received a green card (visa) so they could have access to the wrong portals which are the portals of the kingdom of darkness. They are limited to certain powers and revelations interacting with demonic entities.

Nevertheless, they use this to their advantage by serving the devil. These are opposers to the church and the spiritual things of God. Thus, this is where spiritual warfare is engaged. These individuals will still have an opportunity to repent before they exit this physical world, as long as the breath is still in their nostrils, and they have not blasphemed against the Holy Spirit. They would be obliged to ask Almighty God to forgive them of their sins, relinquish the 'green card' access to the dark world, and become citizens of the kingdom of God! If they decide to keep on being an opposer until death, then there will be no hope, and they will become permanent citizens of the kingdom of darkness.

Most unbelievers who could care less about what's happening in the spirit world are often caught in spiritual warfare without even knowing it. Many walk around daily, complaining they have no luck in life. They failed in almost all aspects. Little did they know that they were caught in a spiritual warfare. Often, God caused misfortune because He wanted to grab someone's attention. He will allow misfortune for that individual to pay Him some attention. This is because he intends to change the person's life and perspective and to bring them into a better place and standing with Him. He will create 'weary steps' that cause you to run to the altar or the foot of the cross! If God had called you from the womb, like Jeremiah (which means that you belong to Him), He will cause havoc in your life until you have no other choice but to surrender!

When God is dealing with an individual one and one, no one can help him- not even the Devil himself! We see what happens when one of God's prophets becomes disobedient, almost costing him everything- even his own life! The prophet Jonah was called to go to Nineveh (the capital of ancient Assyria) to warn the citizens of this city of their wickedness. Jonah chose another route, and that is to rebel against God- it almost cost him his life. We can conclude that no one can escape the clutches of God. If you are reading this book and you feel the call of God on your life, please don't be hesitant; drop everything you are doing right now, fall on your knees (if you can), repent of your sins, and ask Him to come into your heart. In addition, find a sanctuary that upholds the apostle's doctrine (the baptism in Jesus's name and the infilling of the Holy Ghost), and you shall be saved.

The armor that a child of God donned is both offensive and defensive. When fighting a spiritual battle with the proper armor, the child of God can't be defeated. No power can stand against the Holy Spirit of God when we go in Jesu's name. Before the battle began, devils and demons would be scampering away, shaking and trembling. This is because they cannot stand the presence of Almighty God. When Jesus shows up, these rebels instantly feel the red-hot heat of hell!

> *And when He comes to the other side into the country of the Gergesenes, there met Him two possessed with devils, coming out of the tombs, exceeding fierce so that no man might pass by that way. And behold, they cried out, saying, what have we to do with thee, Jesus, thou Son of God? Art, thou come hither to torment us before the time?*
>
> MATTHEW 8: 28-29

God's people have nothing to fear when we are ascertained that the battle belongs to Him. King David has never lost a fight since he was anointed king. Even when the enemy seems to have the upper hand, David always emerges victorious. Isn't that remarkable?! God will not only shield and protect you, but He will also fight your battle. God intervening and defeating the adversary proves that we belong to Him. Oftentimes, the enemy influences our own flesh and blood to come against us fiercely with all sorts of carnal weapons to try and break us. However, we must remember that the battle is not ours; it belongs to God.

Thou shalt not be afraid for the terror by night; Nor for the arrow that flieth by day; Nor for the pestilence that walketh in darkness; Nor for the destruction that wasteth at noonday. A thousand shall fall at thy side, and ten thousand at thy right hand, But it shall not come nigh thee. Only with thine eyes shalt thou behold and see the reward of the wicked. Because thou hast made the LORD, which is my refuge, Even the most High, thy habitation; There shall no evil befall thee, Neither shall any plague come nigh thy dwelling. He shall give His angels charge over thee, to keep thee in all thy ways. They shall bear thee up in their hands, Lest thou dash thy foot against a stone.

Thou shalt tread upon the lion and adder: The young lion and the dragon shalt trample under feet. Because he hath set his love upon me, therefore will I deliver him: I will set him on high because he hath known my name. He shall call upon me, and I will answer him: I will be with him in trouble; I will deliver him and honor him. With a long life, I will satisfy him and shew him my salvation.

PSALM 91:5-16

So, we see the comprehensive protection God places over and around His beloved. He gave us the armor and the weaponry, but He is the one that fights the battle! What an awesome God He is! There is none to be compared with Him. Nothing can defeat us when we are armored up in Christ Jesus. Demons and devils scampered away when we freshly left the boot camp of fasting, praying, and seeking God and headed straight for the battlefield! The first time Almighty God fought my battle and defeated the enemy; I didn't have to think twice about running onto the battlefield afterward. As long as God is with us, all adversaries must back down. When you stand up for God and His righteousness, He will throw your enemy down before you. I assure you that you will see it before your very face.

CHAPTER 9
RISING ABOVE LIFE'S GIANTS

There are so many roaring sounds around us today that if we are not careful, we will soon fall into intimidation. On that note, what sound will you submit to today - the sound of a tyrannical ruler or Almighty God? As I write, many individuals are lying down, playing dead, and rolling over, submitting to the enemy's command. Looking the other way while the heavenly father beckons us to turn to Him will lead to self- destruction. God's power is the greatest power anyone can ever reckon with- and I say this without apology. If you doubt that statement, think about anyone who pulls the sun out of its place every day from the beginning of time without failing or anyone else who can prevent the nights from coming. Can you think of anyone yet? Well, just as I have felt - there is no one else.

Now, if God is the greatest power, then we should never be afraid of the intimidating sound of the evil one. Who can defeat the purpose or the power of God? If He tells you to use what you have (It doesn't matter what it is) to destroy the works of your enemy, then he knows that it will work. Why? Because He is the compelling force behind it! How could David, the son of Jesse, take a simple catapult with a stone and slay a giant that was fully armored, almost ten feet tall, and had been an experienced warrior from his youth? It's got to be with the assistance of some supernatural being - God Himself. In life's experience, we all know it takes extreme training or practice, sometimes accompanied by great skillfulness, to attempt a challenging task for the first time and succeed.

We do not know how long David was in training to be that accurate. We know that David's opponent had been in training since he was a youth. Moreover, he was no easy 'pushover.' He was a giant. There is no telling the number of men this monster had probably killed in battle or training. The sound of this giant alone caused Israel's army to cower. Undoubtedly, David had a helper that was unlike any other. No man, beast, or any dark forces can ever dare match up to him. Yes, our God is a matchless one. On that note, I am pressed to ask, what, who, and where is that giant in your life? Have you been intimidated by his size? Do you run for cover each time you hear his voice? Well, now is the time to fight back. It would be best if you first acknowledged that you are not alone. There is a supernatural being that makes and controls all giants. Now, you must invite Him into your life as a friend. Trust me, He is an expert on bullies.

Often, individuals bear some unnecessary burdens, and their minds are conditioned that there is no hope. They heard that giants were among them - in their cities and villages, even plaguing their homes. Cancer, diabetes, high blood pressure, low blood pressure, anemia, kidney disease, heart disease, lung disease, blood disease, liver disease, heart disease, and many other giants accompanied by their relatives uninvitedly invade our lives, space, time, and again. Time out for that! First, let us gird our minds up; we must protect our heads. These giants could cause traumatizing blows. Worst if your helmet (the helmet of salvation) is not in place. Put on your full armor - the whole

RISING ABOVE LIFE'S GIANTS

armor of God. Then, now launch a counterassault against these giants.

This is where my SPAF (Study, Pray, And Fast) strategy is at its best. I will hit them with a jab, then a hook- SPAF, SPOF (Supernatural Power of Fortification)! I will elaborate more on these two further on. Remember, for those enlisted in the army of Almighty God, He is the One who decides when the battle is over. Moreover, we've made a vow that we will be faithful to Him until death. Knowing these facts, nothing can take us out before the time. The giants may roar, but we have been designed to be giant slayers. God made us who we are so that we can become who he intended us to be, and that's the fact, my friend. Let's go slaughter some giants that are trying to destroy our destiny.

Many individuals feel bad about themselves and their state of being, especially when facing certain circumstances. The oppressor of our souls, the devil, is a lying and deceptive entity. Moreover, that's what he does all day. This is why our minds must be renewed. The enemy is after the minds of every individual in this world, and it is our choice whether to allow him access. We have realized that many have already given up and have been quietly destroyed.

However, there is hope in Jesus Christ for those willing to submit their lives to Him. The Bible states that we should draw near to Almighty God, and He will in turn draw near to us:

Resist the devil and he shall flee.

JAMES 4:7-8

That tells me that we must have some desire for God to step in and take control. It's His desire for us to live and thrive. Don't buy into the lies of the adversary that came to kill, steal, and destroy!

Abundant life awaits those who are willing to surrender all to Jesus! No matter what issues you may face, Jesus remains the only Solution. You may want to try other ways to solve your problems, but the Solution remains the same. Jesus has long orchestrated this, even before the most intelligent man was born, that He Jesus is and will forever be the only solution to man's problems. So, what are you going to do now? When we try to solve our problems alone, they will only get worse! Why? We don't always have the correct answers or solutions because we do not know everything about life's circumstances. However, there is a God that cares. When we understand who Jesus is, we will cast our cares upon Him.

Notwithstanding, there will be some lonely and dreary days in our lives that try to dictate to us that life isn't worth living. How we respond to those circumstances will determine the outcome of our fate. Thus, having the right attitude to life's issues is paramount. Overcoming is the game's name, and with God taking control of the wheel, we can rest assured that it will be all right.

Too many of us throw in the towel when deliverance is about to happen. Some gave up too quickly or too soon and, as a result, cast a shadow of doubt on the ability of their Creator to do the impossible. Impatience has robbed many individuals of their salvation. As a result, an individual who is too shallow in their Christian Walk will soon be toppled over by the slightest wind that blows in their direction. They'll eventually forsake their little faith in God and pursue other solutions. However, when the temporary fix or patch fails, they become bitter and miserable for the rest of their lives.

Those of you outside (of the gospel) looking in, do you want to ride the waves of freedom and happiness for the rest of your life? Do you want abundant life in Him? Then give Jesus everything you've got. You have nothing to lose but sin, shame, and disgrace. Your heavenly Father will not accept just a part of you but the whole. He surrendered all by giving Himself up on an old, rugged cross.

Likewise, He expects us to give Him our all. Only then will you see your life begin to make sense. The word of God declares that if we seek Him with all our hearts, we will eventually find Him.

It doesn't matter what kind of curve ball life throws at you. The critics may say that there is no hope for you. You may feel rejected, neglected, downcast, and even dehumanized and ostracized. However, that's the moment your Creator has been waiting to show up and show off His glory in your life. He will rush in, pick up your broken pieces, assemble them, and make them new again. He will turn your darkness into a brand-new day. Many of us, growing up, must have heard the same story repeatedly- and most must have applied it to our lives and had fantastic results. However, if any of us reading this book may doubt that these sayings are merely cliche or a fantasy, I dare you to challenge God on them and then share your results and testimony later! Many wait until they reach the last end of their rope to try Jesus and see if He can solve their problems.

The enemy of our souls will go above and beyond to try and stop anyone from entering the throne room of Christ. The privilege and benefits he lost from being in the presence of God have fallen on us. Therefore, Satan is not pleased with humans. He is here to steal, kill, and destroy. No doubt, he is doing a great job so far! While many could ignore that there is an opposing entity, those aware and awakened are not backing down. These are the ones whose eyes are lit. If your eyes are not spiritually lit, you won't be able to see what the enemy is doing in the spirit realm. Thus, you would be easily led, even to utter destruction, if not rescued in time. We need someone or something much greater and more powerful than the giants we face regularly in our lives.

Sadly, so many will miss out because of oversights or bypassing the solution. It takes a divine intervention to overcome and rise above life's giants. It wasn't God's will for us to be continuously burdened and filled with fear daily. The cycle must be broken. Our heads should be lifted high and not be hanging down because of anxiety and distress. If you are feeling downcast, open your mouth and shout Jesus! Why? Because at the name of

Jesus, everything must come under subjection. Every giant must come down low. Now, my friend, are you ready to slay some giants? Do you want to live among giants yet not be fearful? We wouldn't likely be rid of some giants, but God will give us the grace to live with or among them.

By now, all of us should realize that life is not an easy street. If we try to take on the pathway of life alone, we'll soon find ourselves wandering down the wrong path, which can lead to disaster. Moreover, we wouldn't have someone to help us in our time of need- when giants appear to discourage and block our path. A giant called cancer may suddenly appear, or high blood pressure and diabetes, to name a few. With Almighty God taking the wheel, there would be a vast difference. He knows pretty well how to handle giants. Someone said the 'bigger they are, the harder they fall!' Despite anything that may happen in your life, it's not the end until God claims it to be so. If God says nothing about it, nobody can do anything about it. Indeed, He has the final say. If He says stop, everything must come to a halt; if He says go, everything must keep moving! A friendly reminder: He is in total control! And if He is in total control, those giants have nothing on us. He will enable us to walk on water and not sink, tread on scorpions and not be bitten, drink any deadly thing and not be hurt, etc.

Fighting life's giants sometimes requires help from spiritual leaders, a friend, or even family members who are God-fearing individuals. The word of God declares that one shall chase a thousand, and two shall put ten thousand to flight. When the children of God unite, there is no telling of the impact this would have on the kingdom of darkness. This could result in a ripple effect that enables many strongholds to be broken, and souls delivered to the honor and glory of Almighty God. Giants will always be there, no doubt, but we have someone far greater than giants living inside us- Jesus Christ, the only potentate. No matter what the giants of life throw at us, our God is more than able to care of His own.

The bullying and the oppression that cause humanity to cower will soon be over, especially for those who wait for Jesus Christ. Many times, the enemy of God's people tried to get rid of them entirely but without success. To utterly be rid of a tree, one must destroy its roots. With God being the root of His people, it takes an individual of total insanity to take on that challenge! The adversary is no match to the Creator of Heaven and Earth. The Devil is a creature constantly in fear and panic because of his irreparable rebellion. The very presence of God causes these entities to go insane!

When you know the God of the universe, there is nothing to fear. You can rest assured that everything will be alright. Demonic entities will be subject to you instead of you under their wicked and oppressive bondage. It's time to rise above these unscrupulous so-called giants and claim what God promised His beloved. There are only two options: We can either be with God and come out victorious or succumb to the wiles of the enemy and be enslaved for eternity. There is no in-between in this matter. There are only two opposing entities battling for the souls of humanity. Which side will you choose? Make your selection wisely, for eternity is a long time.

It is imperative to know that God doesn't automatically decide where we go (eternally) while we are still alive- He gave us the choice to choose. Moreover, He gave us exceptional intelligence that enabled us to decipher most of life's complex situations. Not only did He provide us with intelligence, but he has designed us with a void that only He can fill. Seeking another alternative to fill that void can be detrimental. When that void is not filled with what it was designed for, it attracts outsiders. This is where the problem begins. At first, it may not seem to be important (which was the impression given to Eve by the Devil to disobey God's command in the Garden of Eden), but the consequences can be catastrophic! Notwithstanding, humans tried to fill that (godless) void by making all kinds of ungodly and corrupt decisions. These giants of self- gratification eventually take a toll that is sometimes bad beyond reform.

We must carefully make the right choices, especially regarding our spiritual future. While watching a preaching sermon on social media, I overheard the preacher saying that what one sees on the outside is not the real individual. The actual individual is the 'inward man' or the soul. However, the 'outward man' (the flesh) always thinks about self-gratification. Now, humans tend to feed 'the outward man' all its desires, knowing not that old Mr. Flesh is only temporal (going back to dust) and will not be going over into eternal life. So, while the inward man, which is more vital, is starving, the outward man is being well-fed. This is the total opposite of living for eternal life.

The inward man must be fed good, righteous, and spiritual things to propel him into kingdom fellowship with God. When all is in sync with the spiritual things of God, then we will become overcomers. Many desire and desperately long to slay the giants, causing havoc in their lives, but are not yet in a proper position. Slaying giants are not as easy as it seems. Some situational giants and entities seem so big that it takes rigorous training (prayer, fasting, and engaging God's word) to floor these beasts. We are warriors of the cross; thus, we must follow suit. The minute we take lightly who we are, the adversary will quickly choose this opportunity to try and defeat us.

Someone once stated that an eagle does not have a chicken mentality. Although these birds may seem identical in appearance, there are stalking differences. An eagle's beak is much larger, more curved, and sharper. Its claw-like feet are much larger and sharper, and its wings are much larger and longer. Moreover, the characteristics of these two are different. Now, one may ask: "Why are these two similar in appearance but vastly different? The answer is simple: one was made to inhabit the ground, and the other was made to inhabit the skies. The eagle is more like a predator than a prey. Its nest is perched way up in the tallest trees possible or the cleft of a high mountainous rock. This remarkable flying creature's feet rarely touch the ground, and if it does, it's only to snatch a hefty meal and swoop back up swiftly. While the chicken is in the coup or probably somewhere on the ground scratching for food, the eagle will always be above soaring.

We were called to be God's eagles. When we soar to specific heights, we should be able to see things in the far distance- things in the future, such as snares and traps set by the wicked One to destroy us and our families. Now, as an eagle would, we should swoop down (in prayer, fasting, and engaging the word of God) to destroy and dismantle the enemy's scheme. Many giants are lurking daily, waiting for an opportunity to launch an attack. However, if we don our armor and our sword is girded up, those giants cannot prevail. Slaying giants should be a norm for God's warriors, not a 'once-upon-a-time' thing. If it's only once in a lifetime, as a child of God, I've ever slain a giant, then I would not consider myself a real warrior. With so many giants targeting and pouncing upon the people of God, it's impossible to thrive spiritually and not have these entities under our feet through prayer, fasting, studying, and the power of the Holy Ghost. To say the least, the spiritual war never ceased!

In fighting life's battle, compromising is not an option. God told King Saul to destroy all the Amalekites, one of the archenemies of Israel, but instead, Saul spared the king's life (of all persons) and a considerable portion of their possessions. Now, God was very displeased at this. It was these same Amelikites that tried to prevent Israel from passing through to the promised land. God hasn't forgotten what they have done and therefore intended to punish them for their hostility against His people, Israel. The instructions seemingly sound simple to Saul, but it is essential to know who gave the orders and to carry them out accordingly. However, Saul's failure to carry out God's instructions eventually cost him, his, and his son's life later.

When God set His word forth, He is serious about it fulfilling its purpose:

> *For as the rain cometh down, and the snow from heaven, and returneth not thither, but waterreth the earth, and maketh it bring forth and bud, that it may give seed to the sower, and bread to the eater: so shall my word be that goeth forth out of my mouth: it shall not return unto me void, but it shall accomplish that which I please, and it shall prosper in the thing whereto I sent it.*

ISAIAH 55:10-11

No giants can overturn God's word. "Why?" Because His words are spirits that go forth and execute what He commands. God told His people that no weapon formed against them shall be prosperous, and every tongue that rises up against them shall be condemned in judgment. When we delve into the Scriptures, we can see that as long as God's people trust and obey Him, He'll always show up to give them victory over their enemies. Who wouldn't want a God like that to fulfill all their needs? When we were estranged from Almighty God, these benefits were limited because we weren't totally in sync with Him.

However, Jesus came and restored all that we have lost. Yes, there is no more excuse, my friend. The veil has split open, and we can boldly go to the throne of grace to find help in time of need. We can live above all life's circumstances just by connecting to the kingdom of God. Serving God may seem challenging to most of us, but we can all agree that it has many benefits. Who else can feed, clothe, shelter, heal, and protect you like God? No one else can. God is still yearning for all of humanity to be reconciled and turn to Him, who is the source of our very existence. However, it behooves us to love and serve Him for who He is, not for the benefits. God has repeatedly proven that we are helpless and hopeless without Him.

Know ye that the LORD, He is God: It is He that hath made us, and not we ourselves; We are His people and the sheep of His pasture.

PSALM 100:3

Many individuals today have the inclination that they can make it on their own. This kind of illusional thought would only lead to self-destruction. Nobody can live without God. The preservation of life (the functionality of the human body) and the very breath we breathe are all found in Almighty God. He speaks, and life happens; he pulls back His breath, and death creeps in. How can one do without Him? Can a bird fly without its wings? God is forever the Boss of the universe! Let's go dig into the pure richness of Almighty God. Shall we?

CHAPTER 10
DEMOLISHING THE KINGDOM OF DARKNESS

In the unseen realm, a battle rages on - a war not of flesh and blood but against principalities, against powers against the ruler of Darkness of this world, against spiritual wickedness in high places. This conflict, which we call spiritual warfare, requires children of God to stand firm, be equipped, and be fully armored. The 'kingdom of darkness' is a term used to describe the entities of satanic forces opposing the 'Kingdom of God,' which is the realm of God's sovereignty and total domain. Understanding and engaging in spiritual warfare is paramount for every child of God to live a life of victory, purpose, and prosperity.

The significance of knowing that a spiritual battle is raging cannot be overstated. It is the very thing that influences the physical world in many profound ways, shaping the course of history, individual lives, and even the very fabric of society. The existence of these forces is not a mere myth or relic of ancient superstition. In the Bible, from Genesis to Revelation, there is concrete evidence of the presence and activities of Satan and his legions of fallen angels. These entities are committed to opposing the will of God (our Creator and Father of all things visible and invisible) and to trap humanity in rebellion and sin, which leads to self-destruction.

Satan, once a high-ranking angel named Lucifer, fell from grace due to pride, aspiring to ascend and pitch his throne above the stars of God. He was eventually cast down, and this fall marked the birth of the kingdom of Darkness. Now, the characteristics of satanic forces are manifold. Their primary intentions are to deceive, to steal, to destroy, and to kill. They seek to corrupt what is pure, to destroy what is good, and to lead souls away from salvation. Understanding the nature of these forces is crucial for believers. These entities are not omnipresent, omniscient, or omnipotent like God. Instead, they operate within the limits of divine allowance, exploiting human weaknesses and societal vulnerabilities to foster chaos, despair, and disobedience. Recognizing their methods and manifestations is the first step in combating their scheme.

Satanic influence in today's world is both overt and subtle. It manifests through ideologies that deny the very existence of absolute truth, promote moral relativism, and undermine the sanctity of life and the family unit. This influence is evident in the widespread acceptance of practices contrary to biblical teachings, the normalization of violence and selfishness, and the growing disregard for spiritual authority and the sacred things of God. Countless times, we've seen the devastating effect of the works of the kingdom of darkness. Now, as we recognize the kingdom of Darkness as an actual entity, it is time for us to arise and engage the enemy of our souls, whose goal is to kill, steal, and destroy.

Despite the formidable presence of these forces, believers are not left defenseless. The holy scriptures affirm that through Jesus Christ, we have the power and authority to subdue and destroy the works of the kingdom of darkness. Jesus' victory on the cross disarmed principalities and powers, triumphing over them openly. Now, children of God are called to enforce this victory, standing firm and donning the whole armor of Almighty God. The authority of the child of God stems from their identity in Christ and the indwelling power of the Holy Spirit. With much prayer, fasting, and studying the word of God, we will be able to discern a satanic plot, resist his evil influences, pull down principalities and powers, shut down his cunning devices, and destroy spiritual wickedness in high places.

The very existence of these dark forces unfolds before our very eyes almost all the days of our lives. The innocent and guilty alike fall victim time and again. Those of us awakened through salvation and by the Spirit of Almighty

God have a task. And that task is to destroy the works of darkness. When Jesus was about to send His disciples out to witness, He told them to think not that He came to send peace but a sword [Matthew 10:34]. Thus, He was trying to tell His disciples that a war was happening in the spirit realm. In other words, when you enlist in this army- the church of the living God- you have entered an active battleground! Proceed with caution! Too many claim to be soldiers of the cross and do not even know what is required for the battlefield. They don't even have a clue that there is a battle raging! They claimed to be enlisted but don't even look like it.

What I am driving at is that this is a different kind of army friend. There is nothing frivolous about salvation or the army of God here on earth. If you are playing regarding your salvation, I am here to tell you that God isn't playing. If you are serious, God is even more grave concerning the souls of humanity. Moreover, the enemy is not wasting time but is trying to devour anyone vulnerable to his assault. So now you see how important it is to be fully armored at all times. The goal is to destroy the devil's kingdom. It is kill or be killed- there is no in-between. Those demons must fall like lightning, and their entities be demolished.

"Now, how do we do that?" Someone might be thinking. Do you remember the SPAF (Study, Pray, and Fast) strategy I mentioned earlier? Firstly, you must sanctify yourself by praying, fasting, and studying the word of God. Secondly, you must believe God can execute His will regarding the situation. The kingdom of darkness can't stand when the presence of God saturates a specific region or territory. With constant violence- that is fervent prayer and fasting combined with studying and exercising (speaking the Word of God by faith) we would soon see the enemy's kingdom crumbling. Yes, my friend, many can attest to this, including myself. I must finally suggest that the Spirit of Almighty God will do the damage if we are in sync with Him.

One of the fatal mistakes of a child of God is swift action without thinking when facing opposition. Knowing who we are and who we belong to can sometimes get the better of us. This is in the sense of a lack of spiritual maturity. When we have not developed spiritually, we will be hastened to be angry, rush into a marriage not approved by God, and the like. Eventually, the result of our actions can sometimes be detrimental. The essence is to wait patiently for our Heavenly Father to point us in the right direction and to be obedient while we wait.

Moreover, hiding the word of God in our hearts is a top priority. God's word can be a weapon of offense and defense against the enemy's onslaught. Often, children of God face dire circumstances, which throw unsettled Christians into confusion. Suddenly, instead of addressing these circumstances through the word of God, we take them into our own hands. We immediately forget everything we learned in Sunday school, Bible Study, and even from the preacher. It behooves us to walk in the spirit so we may not fulfill the lust of the flesh. One of the enemy's frequent weapons he uses against Christian is to catch us off guard or unaware- an ambush kind of tactic! Yes, my friend, that's a sneaky one. However, if he is successful, he will use the same tactics repeatedly; now, it's up to us to be watchful and vigilant.

Some of us are unaware we must repeat the process when we fail in a specific area of our spiritual walk. Until we pass the test, we cannot move to another dimension. Overcoming the kingdom of darkness takes a lot of spiritual strategies and patience. The Bible declares that wisdom is essential in overcoming all life's challenges:

Wisdom is the principal thing; therefore get wisdom: And with all thy getting get understanding.

PROVERBS 4:7

We have all it takes to demolish the kingdom of darkness. Most of the time, the struggle is in the mindset of an individual child of God. If the mind that was in Christ is in us always, there is no telling the amount of victory we will have daily as we seek to destroy the works of satanic entities. Did you know that when a child of God is walking in the spirit, God magnifies Himself in us, which causes demons to scramble and run away? Oh yes, my friend, when the adversary sees us, he doesn't just see an ordinary human. God would magnify our appearance so much that we even look like giants! That's one of the reasons why God's word encourages us not to fear!

The power that Jesus has bestowed on the church has taken a toll on the kingdom of darkness. You cannot know or embrace this truth without understanding deep spiritual things. Before Christ, the adversary had straddled humanity like a witch riding on an old, withered broom! Now, when Jesus showed up, hell started panicking! Immanuel came down, and changes began to take place. The devil didn't like it one bit. He even went to the extent of accusing Jesus of coming to torment or judge them before time. Many individuals do not like changes. For this cause, they would shun the Light and refuse to accept Christ.

However, Jesus' coming was to rescue us from the clutches of the enemy: Satan, death, hell, and the grave. God knows more than we do. Though we were dead in trespasses and sins, we thought we were 'OK.' Now God, who knows everything, knew that we weren't. If He did think otherwise to abandon us like a careless and selfish parent, then we would be somewhere in a dungeon or even a garbage heap left up to demon dogs and satanic oppression; got the picture? In other words, there would be no hope for us in this life or the one to come. Wouldn't you want to thank God for taking time out to come and rescue us?

Now, the adversary didn't expect this sudden turn of events, which shattered his kingdom and left him with a head trauma! The table has turned, and the shackles are falling off! Jesus came to set us free; therefore, who the Son set free is free indeed! [John 8:36]. This should be heralded worldwide- even throughout the city of Rome! Today, there is no excuse for not having complete freedom in God. Otherwise, the issue would be of two things: you either hear the gospel and reject ed it, or you have never heard the good news of the gospel before.

Nevertheless, the door of salvation is open for everyone willing to accept Jesus as their Lord and savior. It doesn't matter what walks of life we are from. Everyone can be free from the wicked clutches of the devil. Now that we are free, we must fight to rescue our loved ones—families, friends, associates, and even our so-called enemies. We should all have one common goal: to defeat that old dragon, Satan, trying to destroy our souls. We can't sit down and fold our arms while the Devil is gobbling up the souls of individuals. Let us be aware that the faking lion is up and about seeking who will be his next prey.

Unfortunately, many souls have been lost simply because they didn't happen to find an approved strategy to win life's battle. If we try to take on this fight alone, the casualties will be numerous and our results futile! To fight this battle, we must be fully armored, with the helmet of salvation, the shield of faith, the sword of the spirit, our loins girt with truth, and our feet shod with the preparation of the gospel of peace. We must put on the armor of God to defeat and overcome the adversary. Again, this kind of warfare is not fought with guns, bombs, knives, swords, or machetes. Evil Spirits cannot die (there is no flesh and blood) but can be bound, restricted, or even punished. Moreover, they can be stripped of their power, dominion, and authority and put under subjection through the power of the Almighty God.

When Jesus came into the coasts of Caesarea Philippi, he asked his disciples, saying, whom do men say that I am? And they said, some say that thou art John the Baptist: Some, Elias; and others, Jeremias, or one of the prophets. He saith unto them, But whom say that I am? And Simon Peter answered and said, Thou art the Christ, the Son of the living God. And Jesus answered and said unto him, Blessed art thou, Simon Bar-Jona: for flesh and blood hath not revealed it unto thee, but my Father which is in heaven. And I say also unto thee, That thou art Peter, and upon this rock I will build my church, and the gates of hell shall not prevail against it. And I will give unto thee the keys of the kingdom of heaven: and

whatsoever thou shalt bind on earth shall be bound in heaven: and
whatsoever thou shalt loose on earth shall be loosed in heaven.

MATTHEW 16: 13-19

One may ask, "What is it to be spiritually bound or loose? Well, in terms of bounding, Jesus was referring to demonic principalities, powers, and entities that oppose, sabotage, and exalt themselves against Almighty God and the things concerning Him. These entities would be bound by the supernatural working of Almighty God. Loosing, on the other hand, are the things (which include people, territories, and regions) bound and held in captivity by these demonic entities. Notwithstanding, wherever there are demonic strongholds, there are always demonic activities such as chaos, violence, uprising, sometimes quietness (which is indicative of demonic entities in stealth mode), and all manner of immoralities.

When we figure out how to fight, we can protect regions, territories, and borders and help snatch our loved ones, including families, friends, and associates, out of the enemy's jaws. Now is the time of salvation! Many oppressed individuals need to be rescued, restored, and delivered. Jesus has already given us the key and the authority over the enemy. Before His ascension, He told His disciples that He had given them power over all the enemy's power! Now that's a serious talk. Knowing the adversary's capability, how do we happen to be more powerful than he is? The big difference, my friend, is the Holy Ghost. Individuals with the Spirit of God living inside them are more than conquerors! Can you name Anything, or Anyone for that matter, that can defeat the Spirit of Almighty God?

Thus, it is up to the child of God to prove to everyone the God they trust and serve. We often embarrassed our heavenly Father (I speak for myself) with the things we allowed the adversary to do, both in our lives and the lives of others. We must learn how to (overcome) fight and destroy all the plots and schemes the enemy launches at us before we can qualify to be gap standers. If our lives are not up to par, we cannot help others to be delivered from the wicked clutches of the enemy. Some warfare is so intense that we must seek God with fervent prayer and fasting. We cannot overcome this without these strategies in place.

And one of the multitude answered and said, Master, I have brought unto thee my son, which hath a dumb spirit, and wheresoever he taketh him, he teareth him: and foameth, and gnasheth with his teeth, and pineth away: and I spake to thy disciples that they should cast him out; and they could not. He answereth him, and saith, O faithless generation, how long shall I be with you? How long shall I suffer you? Bring him unto me. And they brought him unto him: and when he saw him, straightway the spirit tare him; and fell on the ground, and wallowed foaming. And he asked his father, How long is it ago since this came unto him? And he said of a child. And oftimes it would cast him into the fire, and into the waters, to destroy him: but if thou canst do anything, have compassion on us, and help us.

Jesus said unto him, if thou canst believe, all things are possible to him that believeth. And the straightway, the father of the child cried out and said with tears, Lord, I believe, help thou mine unbelief. When Jesus saw that the people came running together, He rebuked the foul spirit, saying unto him, thou dumb and deaf spirit, I charge thee, come out of him, and enter no more into him. And the spirit cried and rent him sore, and came out of him: and he was as dead; insomuch that many said, he is dead. But Jesus took him by the hand, and lifted him up; and he arose. And when he was come into the house, the disciples asked him privately, why could not we cast him out? And He said unto them, This kind can come forth by nothing but prayer and fasting.

MARK 9:17-29

Most Christians failed miserably because the proper strategies were not in place. No one goes to war without training, so if we fail to prepare ourselves, we have prepared ourselves to fail. However, these disciples were fresh recruits and were still in training. Now, we can see that we often judge folks according to who they hang out with.

The disciples were with Jesus almost all the time of His ministry. The father of the possessed young man must have seen them with Jesus countless times and thus perceived that they, too, could cast out unclean spirits. It seems somewhat embarrassing to some individuals when what they anticipated through the miraculous working of Almighty God didn't work out for them. Many would even attempt to question God and think of abandoning their faith. We must never forget that it will be granted if God approves our request. However, depending on the situation, the request could be granted sooner or later. Now, if he does not approve it, we can do nothing but give Him the glory and honor due. Simply, it wasn't good for us. The scriptures declare that nothing good will He withhold from them that walk uprightly. [Psalm 84:11].

The faith of the disciples and the possessed man's father seems below zero. The disciples had been on the warrior path before. Earlier, Jesus sent them out in twos, and they returned to him rejoicing, for they had seen demons submitting to them through the power of Jesus's name. Now, they are before this high-ranking demon who has decided to put up a resistance. It takes a cutting anointing to handle a stronghold demon. The greater the anointing of a child of God, the greater the fight! The cutting- edge anointing on David's life caused him to charge toward Goliath without fear. Here, it is impossible for us not to see faith and confidence fuse and ignite together! This scenario reminds us that faith in 'action' is honoring and trusting God for who He is.

Without proper training regarding spiritual war, we cannot cast out demons, raise the dead, heal the sick, rescue, restore, and deliver individuals. The disciples didn't know there were high-ranking demons until they inquired, and Jesus revealed it to them. Therefore, it is imperative for new converts in Christ to be taught thoroughly about these circumstances. Despite being given power over all the power of the enemy, the church must be filled with wisdom, especially in dealing with demonic warfare. Satan is a master copycat. God has poured out all the spiritual gifts and heavenly goodies on His bride, the church; However, the adversary provides his version for his followers. It is paramount for the children of God to have the spirit of discernment. The dangerous weapon of deception that the devil unleashes has caused many spiritually blind individuals to be booby-trapped! Many spiritual leaders have been deceived, especially in the last few years (even today) when the nations of this world were mishandled by the Master of deception.

Until now, many have not fully recovered from the onslaught of this great deception. Individuals have even left the church, abandoning their faith. Nonetheless, God was still in control. He allowed this to wake and shake His people out of slumber. The roots of all so-called grounded Christians were discovered—we saw the contrast between the shallow and the deep-rooted. Despite the circumstances in the life of the apostle Paul, he grew to a spiritual level in Christ that drove him to fully declare that For Christ, he is determined to live and die for the same. [Phillipians 1:21]

CHAPTER 11
REVEALING SATANIC DECEPTION

When I stop and think of the word deception, many things come to my mind. The term has many definitions; however, most, if not all, have a negative connotation. According to the Merriam-Webster dictionary, some of these meanings are Quote: 1. 'The act of causing someone to accept as true or valid what is false or invalid.' Unquote. Another definition is quote: 2. 'The fact or condition of being deceived.' Unquote. Understanding these statements, we can assume that we know the term deception. Furthermore, 'deception' is a noun stemming from the root word 'deceive. With all that being said, let us delve into how the enemy uses deception to manipulate and destroy humanity.

The first time we saw Satan as a deceiver was when he appeared in the Garden of Eden. Now, as we know the story well, God our heavenly Father gave Adam strict instruction not to eat the fruit from one tree (the tree of the knowledge of good and evil) which was in the midst of the garden- 'for in the day that thou eatest thereof thou shalt surely die.' When God made Eve from one of the man's ribs, He presented her before him, so they became one: man and wife. All this time, Satan was observing all things that were unfolding. One minute, he spied, and he saw a man. The next minute, he saw another being also, a woman. This time, he pounced because the man wasn't as approachable as the woman. Moreover, she had gotten second-hand instructions (Adam had told her what God had said about the tree in the midst of the garden).

One day, as Adam was away from the presence of his beauty, the serpent approached Eve.

Yea, Hath God said Ye shall not eat of every tree of the garden?" And the woman said unto the serpent, We may eat of the fruit of the trees of the garden: But of the tree which is in the midst of the garden, God hath said, Ye shall not eat of it, neither shall ye touch it, lest ye die." And the serpent said unto the woman, Ye shall not surely die: For God doth know that in the day ye eat thereof, then your eyes shall be opened, and ye shall be as gods, knowing good and evil:

GENESIS 3: 1-5

Looking back at this scenario, we can see many things going on. Firstly, the woman got second-hand instructions that she wasn't firm on. She told the serpent, "Neither shall ye touch it, lest ye die." That was an add-on to what she was told. Can you say overwhelming curiosity along with a mixture of longing and empathy? Well, she ran into the right person, unfortunately. He (the Serpent) told her exactly what she wanted to hear!

Moreover, Satan had his agenda. Have you ever seen someone with such great hatred for another that they seek others to side with them? Yes, that's the spirit of the Devil himself. Satan's agenda was not only to deceive man to rebel against God, his Maker, but for humanity to have great hatred for Him also. Unfortunately, this conniving beast was triumphant but temporarily:

And when the woman saw that the tree was good for food and that it was pleasant to the eyes, and a tree to be desired to make one wise, she took of the fruit thereof, and did eat, and also gave unto her husband with her; And he did eat.

GENESIS 3:6

And we know the story well. Eventually, the man (and his wife) were driven from the garden lest they put their hands to the 'tree of life' and become default in their sins forever.

So, the deception of the enemy caused the downfall of humanity. Humans now have access to the knowledge of the good and dark sides of life like never before! Humans went and deceived each other time and again, causing hatred, violence, jealousy, murder, and all sorts of sinful acts. Thus, throughout the ages (from the time of Adam) up to this point, all types of deception plague man's life. However, God had a plan from the beginning of time- that is, to rescue man from hell and the power of the grave. Knowing that the adversary would try to thwart the destiny of humanity, He prepared Himself as the lamb slain from the foundation of the world. That was a tremendous blow for the Devil and his entities. This is because God proved Himself as the true shepherd (the only owner), and because of his profound and inexplicable love for the sheep (humanity), He gave Himself up for us. What an incredible story!

The Holy Scripture declares:

> *But God commendeth His love toward us, in that, while we were sinners, Christ died for us.*

> ROMANS 5:8

That, my friend, not only threw the devil into confusion but also exposed him as an imposter! The enemy had us (all humanity) in sin's bondage and deception for so long that when salvation (Jesus or Jehovah is salvation) appears, many of us become immune. The deception dealt a tremendous blow, but how many of us knew that His (God's) grace was greater? I feel a shouting in my feet as I write this part! Again, the devil had miscalculated badly! For this cause, he is relentless in destroying humanity. Now, sons of God, are you ready to fight back or lay down and die? Either way, Jesus will be waiting on the other side when the smoke is cleared.

After deceiving humans for so long, this daredevil confronted Jesus in the 'wilderness of consecration.' Jesus, after being baptized (as a mandatory example) by John the Baptist, was in the wilderness for forty days and nights in consecration. Almost at the end of His consecration (when His body was weak and He was hungry), guess who showed up? - The devil, of course. How many of us know that this coward's most excellent opportunity to destroy us comes at our weakest point? Yes, we all can attest to that fact. Think about that particular time you were feeling down, weak, depressed, and broken-hearted, and he sent an agent to tempt and destroy your reputation, or further when you were at the store, temporarily disabled and couldn't walk properly, and some thief tried to snatch your purse! There are countless situations where the enemy uses these circumstances to his advantage.

However, Jesus's situation was no different. Here Jesus was, in the wilderness, fasting and praying, and Satan showed up. Earlier, he addressed an instruction given by God to His beloved children in the Garden of Eden. Now, this time, it was about Jesus being hungry. It was none of his business in the first place, anyway. It's like that snooping neighbor who always has an agenda and is looking for trouble. He began to say:

If thou be the Son of God, command that these stones be made bread.

MATTHEW 4:3

Now, Jesus wasn't interested in taking instructions from this rebel whose intention was to kill, steal, and destroy. So, with that being said, He hit him (that old Serpent) under his belt with the Word of God:

It is written, Man shall not live by bread alone, but by every word that proceedeth out of the mouth of God.

MATTHEW 4:4

We now see the difference between the two confrontations. Jesus used the word of God, while Eve used her thought process. Thus, ensuring that what we hear matches what Almighty God's word says is essential. In the book of Colossians, Paul writes:

> *Beware lest any man spoil you through philosophy and vain deceit, after the rudiments of the world and not after Christ.*

COLOSSIANS 2:8

Suppose an individual is careless of what they hear and see. In that case, they will be tossed into utter confusion- and even become a notorious talebearer! Furthermore, there will be no solid footing, only slippery ground and disappointments. The devil didn't stop there, however; he went as far as to persuade Jesus to worship him. Can you say daredevil to the utmost?! Lucifer, all the time of his life (and all the angels in heaven), knew nothing else but to worship God; now, suddenly, he wanted to be worshiped. He must have drunk some hard liquor one day, forgot that he was merely a creature, and went haywire! Now, most, if not all, of today's society is infected by this obnoxious disease. Idols are everywhere, and if we don't walk circumspectly as children of God, we will be tripping over ourselves and them, too!

Another trick of the enemy is influencing an individual to have a narcissistic air about them. "Whatever you meant by that? "Someone may ask. Have you ever encountered or seen someone whose ego is so big that there is no room for their brain anymore? Well, this is what our present-day society has become as a result of egotism and selfish behavior -brainless! The potential to think and rationalize circumstances through intelligence and God's word is nonexistent. All that is found is a hoarding of junk- idols! Yes, the adversary had severely damaged our society. In today's world, as a result of narcissism, everyone wants to be worshipped by someone! When the self is unsatisfied with being egotistic, it seeks outside attention or worship. The result always turns out negative, and someone or some individuals eventually get hurt. Thus, our enemy continues the cycle of deception through manipulation. As a starving man desperately hunting for food, the Devil is out and about seeking who will be his next victim.

The master of deception has been everywhere, both high and low. Those who understand spiritual warfare have seen and experienced the enemy's cunning and crafty workings. In a desperate bid for control and power, he manipulates and corrupts entities like governments, cooperatives, institutions, and even the very church (if possible) of the living God. Please make no mistake; he is the true master of deception. No one is exempt. The Holy Scripture declares that the devil will masquerade as an angel of light to deceive an individual who may be unaware of his trickery. Unbelief is one of the weaponry of the devil. If Satan can get individuals to reject the word or even denounce the very existence of God, then he would be triumphing.

When clouds of doubt and skepticism seem to infiltrate our minds, it's a good time to introspect and reason with our God-given intelligence. Even nature itself is screaming at us that there is a God. However, the adversary will want us to believe otherwise- even though he believes there is only one God! [James 2:19]. Now, do we see the deception and insanity of this creature? We cannot afford to be naive and fall prey to the wiles and trickery of demons and devils. God overlooked our ignorance because of the undeniable evidence around us. Anywhere we go in this world, something or someone is declaring the glory of Almighty God. His presence is inescapable. The signs are everywhere:

The heavens declare the glory of God, And the firmament showeth his handywork.

PSALM 19:1

Now, the devil knew this as a fact, but he will try to convince many of us (who are ignorant of the spiritual things of God) otherwise. The skies that hang over us continuously (from the beginning of time) never end, and there are no signs of wear and tear! Think about it! Each morning, we awake, we live to see a new day. There's got to be somebody somewhere constantly being mindful of us- the Lord, God Almighty, who made heaven and earth. God is love; we can see it in the things He made for our benefit. Not only can we see these things, but we can also see His patience toward us, and His love causes Him to suffer long, not willing that any should perish but that all should come to repentance. The Devil, on the other hand, desires for us to perish with Him. Having no hope or chance to return to his former glory, he intends to deprive us of the inheritance we attained through the blood of the Lamb- Jesus Christ of Nazareth. Many individuals have already refused to surrender their old filthy garments of a sinful lifestyle yet still anticipate a tremendous and glorious eternity. This is delusional, and it comes straight from the belly of hell!

And as it is appointed unto men once to die, but after this the judgment: so Christ was once offered to bear the sins of many; and unto them that look for Him shall he appear the second time without sin unto salvation.

HEBREWS 9: 27-28

Self-deception is one of the biggest hindrances in the life of an unbeliever. If individuals could deceive themselves, then they would likely deceive others likewise. The days are here where many shall deceive many, and many shall be fooled by many! We often see and hear this in the news media more than ever. Often, folks who love to hear something new or commit themselves to gossiping become victims. This also is a weapon used frequently against humanity by the kingdom of darkness. Satan intends to target and discover everyone's weaknesses, shortcomings, and secret faults and manipulate them to his advantage. If one's addicted to partying, he will indeed present the latest events and reveling to you before you even think about it.

The enemy's greatest delight is to catch us off guard. The moment we become lapse; he'll seize that opportunity to inflict our souls.

The adversary will plague us with all kinds of unnecessary addictions. Initially, he would let it seem excellent and harmless, but the backlash is like a deadly poisonous snake in the end! Does anyone understand or is aware of the Devil's scheme? In these trying times, we must adorn ourselves with the whole armor of God. The word of God stated that if it is possible, Satan would have deceived the very elect:

> *For there shall arise false Christs, and false prophets, and shall shew great signs and wonders; insomuch that, if it were possible, they shall deceive the very elect.*

MATTHEW 24:24

Now, let us elaborate a little more on this. If the enemy wanted to deceive the very elect, what more outsiders, or let's say, unbelievers? This kind of deception is more pronounced than the ordinary. It means there is no return to the former state once deceived. For example, those deceived by accepting the 'Mark of the Beast' will be lost forever. The mark is the final confirmation of the individual decision to spend their long eternity in hell. To some, this is a very sensitive and touchy subject, but we must face reality and emphasize the truth when and where it is needed most. Let's face it: certain deceptions are detrimental.

Jesus didn't just show up on earth for us to have a ball or a pity party! He came for one reason and is: to get us out of the bondage of sin, thus preventing us from going to hell. That's it! If God can orchestrate such a plan that His efficacious blood would be shed to rescue humanity, it must be critical! We can't afford to miss out on the promises God gave to our forefathers long before the Lamb (Jesus Christ) appeared. When the sacrificial Lamb was slain, the door was opened for whosoever will accept the invitation to be saved from the wrath that is to come. Now that the good news (the gospel of God) has been borne, there is no excuse not to be saved.

For the grace of God that bringeth salvation hath appeared to all men, teaching us that, denying ungodliness and worldly lusts, we should live soberly, righteously, and godly in this present world.

TITUS 2:11

The Scripture declares that the Word is not far from us for us to find an excuse to say, who shall go and fetch it that we might know? Therefore, there is no pardon for not accepting such great salvation.

But the righteousness which is of faith speaketh on this wise, Say not in thine heart, Who shall ascend into the heavens? (That is, to bring Christ from above:) or who shall descend into the deep? (That is, to bring up Christ again from the dead.) But what saith it? The word is nigh thee, even in thy mouth, and in thy heart: that is, the word of faith, which we preach; that if thou shalt confess with thy mouth the Lord Jesus, and shalt believe in thine heart that God hath raised him from the dead, thou shalt be saved.

ROMANS 10:6-9

We can only miss out on this great promise if we fail to comply with God's rules and ordinances. God's commandments are not grievous, but His salvation is joy unspeakable and full of glory; the other half has not yet been told. We can be happy in Christ while we look and wait for that blessed hope. Challenges will come, but we are more than conquerors. Are you excited to meet your God? If not, gird up your loin, lift the hands that hang down, strengthen those feeble knees, 'quit ye like men,' and be strong, for the Lord your God is about to appear. The enemy will always be throwing distractions our way to hinder us from making it to the finishing line.

However, we should not look to the right or the left but keep our eyes on the prize. It won't be long before we reach destiny's shore. As we move on in this life, Satanic deceptions will only intensify. These subtle devices orchestrated by devils have already swallowed up many.

Thus, it calls for a spiritual awakening. Without Almighty God revealing spiritual things to us, we would become as deaf and dumb animals without any sense of direction.

The Devil is out to get those who are committed to unravel and destroy his deceptive schemes. He tries to frustrate us in many ways. However, we should be more determined than ever to defeat his purpose. Too many souls are held in chains of darkness. Many won't know this until they wake up on the other side of life, only to discover their souls have been lost. For this cause, God has called us watchmen for those whose souls are ready to perish. Yes, those of us who are already in the kingdom are to be watchers for the souls of men. God has given us the Spirit of power, love, and of sound mind so that we can discern the enemy's wicked deceptions.

In these last days, the deception of the wicked One has dramatically intensified. Children of God who were stalwarts had returned from the faith, giving heed to seductive spirits and doctrines of devils. Sounds familiar? Folks who used to stand for righteousness and defy moral turpitude are now paying homage to the wiles of the enemy. Indeed, we are in the last days. Most can attest to the fact that Satanic deceptions were around long before we even came into existence. But now we see that it has gotten worse over decades and centuries. The final lap is about to happen, and the enemy knows he has but a short time. Some individuals have been deceived into accepting other doctrines and religions besides those preached by the apostles.

> Now, therefore, ye are no more strangers and foreigners, but fellow citizens with the saints, and of the household of God; and are built upon the foundation of the apostles and prophets, Jesus Christ himself being the chief cornerstone; in whom all the building fitly

framed together groweth unto a holy temple in the Lord: in whom ye also are builded together for a habitation of God through the Spirit.

EPHESIANS 2:19-22

It is impossible to make it to the rapture without taking on the name of Jesus Christ in water baptism and being filled with the Holy Ghost. Yes, my friend, the rapture is the next big event on earth. Everything is almost in place now, and the stage is set for the son of Perdition, the antichrist. He cannot show up unless the church is gone! The power of the church is what prevents him from showing up!

As the church (the bride of Christ) disappears beyond the skies, the whole world would be left in chaos. The body of Christ is the only one that keeps back the dark forces of hell from engulfing the world already. As long as the church is here, the power of God is with her. There is nothing impactful the Devil can do until the church leaves. When the church leaves, the power of God is lifted so the enemy will sweep in. Who dares want to be on Earth, then? For the ones that are left behind, it won't be easy. It would be a do-or-die situation. The church will not be here to overpower or subdue any powers coming from hell. Whew! That's a hard pill to swallow.

So, we see how imperative it is to receive Jesus Christ now before 'our number' is called- or before the rapture:

Wherefore (as the Holy Ghost saith, today if ye will hear His voice, Harden not your hearts, as in the provocation, In the day of temptation in the wilderness: When your fathers tempted me, proved me, and saw my works forty years. Wherefore I was grieved with that generation, and said, they do alway err in their heart; and they have not known my ways. So I sware in my wrath, they shall not enter into my rest.) Take heed, brethren, lest there be in any of you an evil heart of unbelief in departing from the living God.

HEBREWS 3:7-12

The spirit of unbelief will take more people down to hell's belly than anything else. Even if an individual believes there is a God and doesn't spare the time to know and accept Him as LORD and Savior, it's considered unbelief. No wonder the apostle James declares in his epistle to the saints that *faith without works is dead.*

JAMES 2:20-26

If one had heard the gospel from a child, had grown, lived to the fullest, died, and exited this world without receiving it, they are still unbelievers. Further, the Bible calls it self- deception because they heard the word but failed to apply it to their lives.

CHAPTER 12
BREAKING STRONGHOLDS

Most individuals reading this book may not be familiar with the term stronghold, and even if they do, how does it apply to the spiritual things of God? First, let us define the term stronghold. In a broad sense, a stronghold is a fortified place or a fortress that offers protection. It can also be defined as a place ravished, captured, and taken captive by an enemy. However, strongholds have a much more nuanced meaning regarding personal development and spirituality. A spiritual stronghold is an attack on the mind that negatively affects the behavior and attitudes of an individual. These can be thoughts of anxiety, negativity, fear, or any belief that contradicts the truth of what is written in the holy scriptures.

Now, when we apply strongholds to spiritual things, we can see an active force working against the progression and productivity of humanity. As stated in an earlier chapter, I mentioned Jesus's arrival on the scene, which triggered an exposure of the enemy's intent to destroy all of humanity. Many individuals today walk around without a clue that they are spiritually bound. Yes, I was one of them, my friend. Nonetheless, 'I went to the church one night, and my heart wasn't right, and something got a hold of me!' That relief- the peace and joy I was looking for happened instantly. I was held firm by the terrible chains of the enemy, and before I knew it, boom! Here comes Jesus. He broke through the enemy's fortress, tore the trap door down, broke off all my chains, and set me free. Glory Hallelujah! You can shout it with me now if you are secluded, lest anyone think you are all nuts! Who cares anyway? After all, God deserves all praises openly and continuously. Combined with His name, praises cause demons to get cold feet and send them scrambling!

So now we understand that when God comes to our rescue, He breaks off every chain and fetter that was put in place by Satan, who was holding us captive. However, he desires to use us through His power to break off strongholds in the lives of others. Nonetheless, we still have many walking around in bondage. Some are even on the brink of committing suicidal acts. Yes, there is a war going on, my friend, and they have got to be bootstrapped on the ground. Many mental illnesses are stronghold. So-called dysfunctional behaviors and violent and reckless attitudes all stem from spiritual strongholds. Do you see that we have work to do? Many people today have a good heart, and when asked what they would like to do for humanity, they often respond with great excitement. But do you know that the very place to begin helping others is helping ourselves first? Yes, fixing ourselves first will enable us to help others fix themselves. We must take care of certain things regarding ourselves before caring for others. An individual who wants to counsel another psychologically cannot be bound Psychologically. What energy do you bring to the table?

When an individual is baptized in Jesus's name, filled with the Holy Ghost (and fire), and living righteously for the living God, he will be mentally prepared to assist his fellow humans in breaking off strongholds. Most strongholds are not easily broken. Therefore, some strategies must be used to approach these kinds of strongholds. The strongholds of brokenness, despair, hopelessness, fear, and depression dig deep down into the core and psyche of their victims. These strongholds can move from one stage to the other regarding severity. For example, the stronghold of oppression could lead to depression, then from depression into possession or even insanity!

While physical strongholds refer to something that can often be seen or touched, such as a fortress or a secured place, spiritual strongholds are intangible. They reside in the mind and spirit, manifesting through our thoughts, actions, and reactions to various situations. Unfortunately, no one is exempt from the strongholds of the enemy. However, thanks be to God, who has given us (those baptized in Jesus' name and filled with the Holy Ghost and fire) the power to destroy the yoke! Addressing spiritual strongholds is crucial for personal growth and spiritual development. These strongholds can hinder our relationship with others, ourselves, and, most importantly, with God. They keep us in bondage and prevent us from living the abundant life that is promised in the holy word of God.

There are many ways in which a stronghold can exist in your life, sometimes unknowingly: Continuous engagement in sin can fortify negative beliefs and behaviors, creating strongholds that bind individuals. Most often, strongholds are passed down through families as patterns of behavior or belief that are learned and replicated across generations. These are sometimes seen as generational curses. The world around us can shape our thinking and beliefs, sometimes in ways that are contrary to God's Word. Materialism, pride, and self-reliance are societal influences that can become spiritual strongholds. The presence of spiritual strongholds can severely impact an individual's life, leading to a disconnection from God, strained relationships, and an overall sense of spiritual bondage. For communities, strongholds can manifest as a collective set of rules, laws, or practices not conducive to God's law and ordinances. Thus, it destroys normal relationships with families and society. This is because it has no moral turpitude regarding Biblical principles.

Throughout the Bible, numerous accounts of individuals and nations faced physical and spiritual strongholds. For example, the Israelites struggled with a stronghold of idolatry, repeatedly turning away from God to worship false gods. Another example is the Israelites' fear and unbelief when faced with certain circumstances in the wilderness, such as thirst, hunger, and even giants. The constant banging of fear, worry, murmuring, and complaint caused an indelible effect seen as a stronghold of unbelief.

So, now that we have explored and investigated the signs and symptoms of a stronghold let's get to how we can break and destroy it in our lives and the lives of our families, friends, and acquaintances. Romans 12:2 emphasizes the importance of renewing our minds with God's word to transform our lives. When an individual accepts Jesus Christ (baptized in Jesus's name and filled with the Holy Ghost), the Bible declares that They have become new creatures; the old or former things are gone, and everything in that individual life has become new. [2 Corinthians 5:17] This means that these strongholds plaguing a person's life are sometimes automatically broken off at the time of conversion.

On the other hand, it became a chronic process where God, through the Holy Ghost, gradually breaks the bond asunder as the individual progresses. Breaking free from spiritual strongholds requires divine intervention and spiritual habits and practices. This process can be challenging but is achievable through steadfast faith, consistent effort, and the support of a faith-based community, such as a church that embraces the true doctrine of the apostles and believes in the supernatural power of Almighty God.

A sober and conscious believer in Christ should honestly begin with a self-assessment to identify specific thoughts, attitudes, or behaviors contrary to God's Word. The individual should Acknowledge these strongholds before God in prayer, craving His intervention to overcome them. Secondly, the believer should focus on constant prayer, asking God to reveal hidden or undetected strongholds and provide strength and wisdom for breaking free of them. Moreover, fasting, studying, and exercising the Word of God is one way to draw closer to God- seeking His intervention and guidance in defeating and overcoming demonic strongholds.

Finally, hearing from those who have overcome spiritual strongholds can be of great encouragement and provide practical insights for those who are bound. Countless individuals were in dire circumstances and through prayer, studying, and fasting, the power of the Holy Ghost shattered the chains and shackles of all kinds of strongholds that had them in bondage. What kind of strongholds are hindering you from progressing right now? Well, what are you waiting for to be free? The word of God declares that whosoever shall call upon the name of the Lord shall be saved. [Joel 2:32, Acts 2:21, and Romans 10:13]. Go ahead now, I dare you to call on Him, for He will surely answer!

I come to observe that many individuals do not have the slightest hint that they are being bound. This is compared to a bird that flew down to get some meal from a makeshift trap, and before it could make its way back out, it was too late. Many folks have been trapped in many ways. Some blindly went into unbecoming forms of agreement that bound them, their loved ones, families, friends, and associates for life. Strongholds are natural; they'll make you do things you don't want to, go places you don't want to go and be in a relationship you don't want to be in, etc. Mental depression, disorder, and derangement are only some of the strongholds of the mind that the enemy implemented to bring it into complete captivity. Now, having been aware of these various types of strongholds, let us begin to do something about it.

Do you have the proper tools for the job? Jesus's name is our authority, the Holy Ghost is our weapon of war, and living righteously is our training camp. Have you been in training lately? If you answer yes to all the above, then you are ready for battle! The devil has implemented spiritual strongholds to manipulate and ensnare many souls. However, by the grace and power God invested in us, we can defeat every form of satanic stronghold. No devil in hell big enough can confront us when we are fully equipped! God will make you into a giant before the enemy. You will grow right before their very eyes. They will come in one way and flee in seven different directions. Do you see the privilege we have in God? His Protection is guaranteed. Even when we weren't in sync with Him and His word, He protected us. What an awesome God to be reckoned with! He will move heaven and earth to rescue us from the enemy.

Many individuals love the benefits of serving the Lord but reject the price we must pay. The Bible tells us that Jesus was up and about doing good, and many pined after Him daily because of what they had seen and heard. However, some of these folks weren't merely following because they loved him or his teaching. They were following because of the material benefits:

The day following, when the people which stood on the other side of the sea saw that there was none other boat there, save that one whereinto his disciples entered, and that Jesus went not with his disciples into the boat, but that his disciples were gone away alone; (Howbeit there came other boats from Tiberias nigh unto the place where they did eat bread after the Lord had given thanks:) when the people, therefore, saw that Jesus was not there, neither his disciples, they took shipping, and came to Capernaum, seeking for Jesus.

And when they had found him on the other side of the sea, they said unto him, Rabbi, when camest thou hither? Jesus answered them and said, Verily, Verily, I say unto you, Ye seek me, not because ye saw the miracles, but because ye did eat of the loaves, and were fillled. Labour not for the meat which perisheth, but for the meat which endureth unto everlasting life, which the son of man shall give unto you: for him hath God the Father sealed.

JOHN 6: 22- 27

It is paramount that when we have been healed, delivered, or rescued (whatever the stronghold was that was broken off us), we follow steadfastly after Jesus lest a worse thing come upon us. We cannot afford to take his grace and mercies for granted.

The enemy has had many of us in bondage for decades; we have been tossed to and fro by demonic strongholds, but now we are free! "Hooray! Hallelujah!" As I exalt the Lord for His great work in our lives, I remembered my uncle-in-law's experience. I recalled that moment when he was looking timid and hopeless. In frantic fear and desperation, he started calling upon the name of Jesus, and eventually, the stronghold was broken off his life. As you read this book, there is no telling the number of individuals under devils' strongholds. Often, we don't necessarily have to go and lay our hands on or touch anyone physically to break strongholds off them, though this is required sometimes. Prayer is a mighty weapon in breaking strongholds. The Bible states that:

The effectual fervent prayer of a righteous man availeth much.

JAMES 5: 16

However, a combo is even more effective- studying (the word of God), praying, and fasting. When a child of God buckles down in fasting, praying, and seeking the face of the Lord, it guarantees that hell's gate will be rattling from a distance. The devils will take note, drop their weapons, and scamper off to a far place. Unity is the key. Sometimes, the children of God lack unity- yes, my friend, even the church itself. Most of the time, the enemy is more uniform than us. They will move in close uniformity and coordination. Their 'Netcom' or communication systems are hotwired! This means they position themselves strategically in a network pattern, trying to execute their diabolical deeds undetected. They constantly go to and fro throughout the earth, hoping to prey on a victim. Do you see the uniformity of the demonic operations here? Unfortunately, many fell prey to these diabolical entities.

Moreover, if one does not know how to fight and push back the enemy's onslaught, they will ultimately be run over. Breaking and destroying strongholds is not easy. Strategies must be put in place to defeat the adversary's destructive plan. Many individuals are under strongholds and are not even aware of them. They go about their business burdened with the spirit of oppression, depression, and, eventually, possession. All these are elements of strongholds.

The darkness enveloping many folks causes them to think that this world is it! There is none like it or any other paradise beyond. Therefore, they display a kind of attitude, not knowing they are spiritually bound. With this, I must say that affiliation with the people and the house of God is imperative. Most will only show up in the house of God when there is a specific event, such as a funeral service for a loved one or an invitation to a wedding. However, lingering in the wilderness of sin for too long can be detrimental.

Some of us understand the blood covering from the Old Testament:

> *And the blood shall be to you for a token upon the houses where ye are: and when I see the blood, I will pass over you, and the plague shall not be upon you to destroy you when I smite the land of Egypt.*

EXODUS 12: 13

That same concept transfers from the physical (Old Testament) to the spiritual (New Testament) when Jesus Christ, the ultimate sacrificial Lamb, shed His blood for us all on Calvary's cross.

Now, we assume that we are safe because some relatives or associates of ours are praying for us and pronouncing a blood covering. Despite this, we cannot take the grace of God for granted. Many times, when Jesus delivered the sick, the mute, and the oppressed, he told them to go and sin no more. It's impossible to live in sin and abound in God's grace. Does that mean that we are not likely to sin? Of course, not; The issue is that we don't practice living in sin once the efficacious blood of Jesus Christ redeemed us. In other words, we strive to be His reflection as we grow into spiritual maturity. Now, when an individual has been delivered from the clutches of sin and the devil's stronghold, they must stay clear, lest they fall back into the same trap. The Wicked one is cunning and will do all he can to bring us back into captivity. In this case, one must be watchful through the Holy Ghost and prayer.

No one is exempt from the onslaught of the enemy. I could care less about how much of a spiritual person you may be. Anyone baptized in Jesus's name and filled with the Holy Ghost and fire can attest to this- especially if they have been on the battlefield for a while. It is true when the scriptures declare that 'experience teaches wisdom.' No matter how careful one tries to walk, the enemy will toss some form of obstacle your way. Enemy aside, even we could be our own stumbling block! When we all understand that we are merely living off God's grace and mercies, we will realize that all our righteousness is as filthy rags! Thus, we are constantly fighting and breaking strongholds of sin. There is no letting up, my friend. The souls of many are on the line.

One of the worst forms of bondage is the stronghold of the mind. The enemy can take possession of an individual mind so that they would not even be conscious of their actions, attitude, or behavior, much less cry out for spiritual help. If they are fortunate, they would be left to the mercy of a praying child of God, with a cutting-edge kind of anointing! Breaking strongholds often requires consistent prayer and fasting. The more a child of God invests in spiritual things, the more positive results they will see. Fasting (along with prayer and studying God's word) is called 'killing the flesh' to empower the inward man- which is our true self! Now, killing the flesh doesn't mean that a person is Physically abusing the body because of hatred for themselves; As was mentioned before, it is a spiritual thing.

No one can explain the supernatural working of Almighty God; we can only believe and then receive it with gratitude. Someone may ask." How do we know it's God? Well, it was promised in His words, and we see it fulfilled just as He says it would. It was impossible for it not to happen because His words are like spirits executing His will in heaven and Earth! God will not give His beloved Children anything that will bring harm to them.

> *Every good and perfect gift is from above, and cometh down from the father of lights, with whom is no variableness, neither shadow of turning.*
>
> JAMES 1:17

The power that the church possesses today cannot be compared with any other. The copycat power that the Devil is trying to impress on humanity is working somewhat, but it won't last long.

The church must put on the whole armor of God, stack up on our arsenal, and run to the battle. Those determined to fight to the death will still be breaking strongholds. One songwriter declares:

> *Then forward still is Jeohvah's will though the billows, dash, and spray. With a conquering tread, we'll push ahead, and He (God) will roll the sea away!*

Strongholds are broken not by might or power but by the Spirit of Almighty God. Our intimate relationship with (YAWEH) God will prompt Him to do anything we request in His name. God loves people, and His desire to intervene in our lives for His love's sake is paramount.

No wonder He came in the form of human flesh to experience what we experience so that He could be touched by the feeling of our infirmities! [Hebrews 4:15] He was God clothed in flesh to relate on our level. It's time to start breaking strongholds, my friend. Even if you've been on the battlefield for a while, Jesus said that the harvest was white, but there were few laborers. Let us bombard the enemy's base, destroy strongholds, and rescue the captives. Someone somewhere is crying out for help. We have what it takes to conquer the adversary and to rescue, restore, and deliver God's people from the clutches of hell. Are you ready for battle?

CHAPTER 13
OVERCOMING THE BEAST OF EPHESUS

The term 'The Beast of Ephesus' is not just a mere phrase but a complex tapestry of history, religion, and culture, deeply entwined with the ancient city of Ephesus itself. This enigmatic 'Beast' often evokes images of monstrous creatures from folklore, yet it represents a far more profound and multifaceted concept in this context. Let us delve into the city that is associated with this mysterious entity. Ephesus's significance in the ancient world cannot be overstated. It was a hub of trade, culture, and religion, famous for the Temple of Artemis-one of the Seven Wonders of the Ancient World. However, its prominence also made it a focal point in the nascent Christian movement, often clashing with pagan traditions. This dichotomy set the stage for the emergence of 'The Beast,' a system (or entity, for that matter, consisting of evil men in high places) that has been studied, checked, investigated, and deciphered through biblical scriptures, most notably in the Book of Revelation.

In Revelation, "The Beast" is not just a creature but a metaphor for persecution, moral decay, and the struggle between good and evil, deeply rooted in the early Christian experiences of adversity and martyrdom. Using the term 'beast' as a metaphor compared to men is not unusual, especially in the Holy scriptures. The book of Psalms declares:

Many bulls have compassed me: Strong bulls of Bashan have beset me round.

PSALM 22: 13

This was David pouring out his complaint to the Lord and pleading for His help because great men were determined to destroy him. We saw Ephesus first mentioned in the book of Acts of the Apostles when Paul arrived in the city (from Syria) accompanied by a pair of new converts- Priscilla and Aquila.

Now Ephesus, nestled in the fertile lands of modern-day Turkey, was not just a city; it was a beacon of civilization, trade, and spirituality. Its strategic location near the Aegean Sea made it a crossroads of trade routes, connecting the East and West. This geographical advantage allowed Ephesus to flourish economically and culturally, attracting artisans, traders, and scholars from across the ancient world. The religious landscape of Ephesus was as diverse as its population, and the city was a testament to human spiritual hunger and architectural grandeur. The Temple of Artemis, one of the Seven Wonders of the Ancient World, symbolized the city's deep-rooted pagan traditions. The city's religious plurality set the stage for the later introduction of Christianity, which would both enrich and challenge the existing spiritual tapestry.

When Christianity was introduced to the Ephesian society, it changed the whole aspect of their political and religious genre. As dark as this society seemed then, the light pierced through that thick darkness of sin and destruction. Mark you, other neighboring cities around and about Ephesus were no different. However, just like in other cities, Ephesus seemed somewhat to catch the eye of GOD. The apostle Paul was the first to bring the gospel to the Ephesians. Before Christianity, Ephesus was filled with many gods. The Ephesians worship a god of fertility, whom they associate with the Greek goddess Artemis and other deities, including the goddess, Diana. So, when the apostles embarked upon Ephesus, they started pushing back against the forces of darkness. This strongly caused the Roman era to bring about significant challenges for the developing Christian community. As the city struggled between this 'New Way' and Roman paganism,

Christians found themselves locked at odds with the official religious and social orders.

The tension between the Christian minority and the dominant pagan practices contributed to the emergence of "The Beast" as a symbol of oppression and conflict, mirroring the broader struggle of Christianity to establish itself within the Roman world. The apostles turned the city of Ephesus upside down by persuading men to salvation (through Jesus Christ, our Lord and Savior) and with many signs and wonders. No doubt, they had faced much opposition and extreme resistance, but because of the power of Almighty God, they could break through strongholds and dismantle the kingdom of darkness.

The Triumph of Light As the sun dipped below the horizon, casting long shadows across the city, Paul stood face to face with beast-like men in the sacred precincts of Artemis' temple. With fervent prayers upon his lips, he invoked the name of the Almighty, calling upon divine intervention to defeat the forces of darkness. In a crescendo of spiritual energy, the Beast was cast down, its hold over Ephesus shattered, and the city bathed in the light of redemption. Legacy of Courage In the aftermath of the epic struggle, Ephesus emerged from the shadows, transformed by the indomitable spirit of the apostles. The cult of Artemis waned, replaced by a burgeoning community of believers drawn to the teachings of the doctrine of Jesus Christ the Messiah. Paul's brave stance against the Beast became etched into the annals of history, inspiring future generations to embrace faith over fear and confront the darkness within and without.

As we reminisced about the apostle's conquest in Ephesus and neighboring cities, what kind of beast is in your life today? Who is winning- are you, through the efficacious blood of Jesus Christ, or are you lying down and playing dead? I hope it is the former, for Jesus will be the focal point of everything when all is said and done. Everything will be brought under His feet. No demons, devils, beasts, or beast-like men could stand against Him! Absolutely none. Some of life's beasts are necessary in that they would drive us to the cross and have us hold on to the horn of the altar. The most dangerous beast is the religious systems and doctrines implemented by devils. The intent is to steer humanity away from this unadulterated gospel to myth and fables. Individuals with a hitchhike spirit will be easily led away (with every wind of doctrine) because of their free will attitude. The wise thing to do is always check the spirits to see if it is of Jesus Christ:

> *Beloved, believe not every spirit, but try the spirits whether they are of God: because many false prophets are gone out into the world. Hereby know ye the Spirit of God: Every spirit that confesseth that Jesus Christ is come in the flesh is of God: And every spirit that confesseth not that Jesus Christ is come in the flesh is not of God: And this is that spirit of antichrist, whereof ye heard that it should come, and even now already is it in the world.*

1 JOHN 4:1-3

The diabolical plan of the adversary is to control territories that are not rightfully theirs. As long as they can hold a region under spiritual bondage, it is better. They become comfortable in that area and deprive humanity of their substance and energy. According to Mathew, the gospel recorded an instance when Jesus entered the territory of the Gergesenes. Immediately, the demonic entity that controlled the region confronted him:

> *And when he has come to the other side into the country of the Gergesenes, there met him two possessed with devils, coming out of the tombs, exceeding fierce, so that no man might pass by that way.*
>
> *And, behold, they cried out, saying, what have we to do with thee, Jesus, thou son of God? Art thou come to torment us before the time? And there was a good way off from them a herd of many swine feeding. So the devils besought him, saying, if thou cast us out, suffer us to go into the herd of swine. And he said unto them. Go. And when they were come out, they went into the herd of swine: and, behold,*

the whole herd of swine ran violently down a steep place into the sea and perished in the waters.

MATHEW 8: 28-32

The prince of Darkness is never willing to leave a region, at least not peacefully. So, we see why he decided to put up a resistance against the servant of God in Ephesus.

Every child of God has a beast to wrestle with. If you are called by the name of Jesus Christ and haven't experienced any resistance against you from the dark world, then you must check yourself. I said it before, and maybe after this, as a reminder that when you have received Jesus Christ as your Lord and Savior, baptized in his name and filled with the Holy Ghost, consider yourself enlisted in a spiritual army- the army of God. Now, all of us should know the duty or the purpose of having an army. Often, an army would engage in serious warfare. Causalities will occur, and the prevailing military will be the victor.

Now, it's essential to know the nature of the army you enlisted in and the fellow soldiers you will interact with. Welcome to your new family! Moreover, you should always make an effort to show up for training in case you should miss something that would save you during enemy combat engagements! The army of God is not an ordinary one. We don't wrestle with flesh and blood but against principalities and powers, the ruler of darkness of this world and spiritual wickedness in high places. In other words, we are fighting against wicked and destructive spirits that are trying to destroy our world and everything in it. No doubt, Ephesus's beast is still around! Seeing that, we can't get rid of this beast until the end of time; we should prioritize overcoming him and assisting others (our families, friends and associates, and even our so-called enemies!) in doing likewise.

This beast has killed (put to sleep) many, both physically and spiritually. Spiritual sleep can be temporary, but physical sleep can be detrimental. When one is physically dead, there is no return. There is still a chance for those who are spiritually dead; We still have time to rescue these lost souls from the clutches of the beast. Are you fired up?! Are you ready? Do you feel holy war running through your blood?

> *For by thee I have run through a troop; And by my God have I leaped over a wall. He teacheth my hands to war, so a bow of steel is broken by mine arms.*

> PSALM 18: 29 & 34

God is willing to empower His children to wage war against the adversary. Moreover, with God on our side, we can't lose!

The 'beast system' we are dealing with today is very crafty and deceptive. Unfortunately, many fellow soldiers who started with a no-retreat, no-surrender, and a non-compromise stance had compromised and eventually became enemies of the cross. The picture here is not to deem anyone perfect cause no one is but God. However, we all should strive for perfection once we leave the arena of being spiritual babes:

> *Therefore leaving the principles of the doctrine of Christ, let us go on to unto perfection; not laying again the foundation of repentance from dead works, and of faith toward God, of the doctrine of baptisms, and of laying on of hands and of resurrection of the dead, and eternal judgment. And this will we do if God permits.*

> *For it is impossible for those who were once enlightened, and have tasted of the heavenly gift, and were made partakers of the Holy Ghost, and have tasted of the good word of God, and the powers of the world to come, if they shall fall away, to renew them again unto repentance; seeing that they crucify to themselves the Son of God afresh, and put him to an open shame. For the earth which drinketh in the rain that cometh oft upon it, and bringeth forth the herbs meet for them by whom it is dressed, receiveth blessing from God: but that*

which beareth thorns and briers is rejected, and is nigh unto cursing;
whose end is to be burned.

HEBREWS 6: 1-8

The beast has been around for a long time, hiding, ducking, and slithering in the shadows. At the very end, God will bring Him into complete exposure, and then all eyes will see that old serpent that deceived the whole world. By then, it would be too late for some individuals who reject the gospel and Jesus Christ, the Truth, the Way, and the Life. While our eyes are open more than ever to the oncoming events according to the Bible, we can rest assured that the way is already paved for the 'Beast' to appear. The Beast, also called 'the Antichrist,' will push up his ugly head, pretending to be the 'Messiah.' He will attempt, with all his might, to suppress and oppress all who oppose him. Many beasts have risen against the People of God before. Still, this last and ultimate beast stampede is Satan's attempt to finish what he started in the heavens- to usurp God's authority and to be the ultimate ruler. The church will be 'taken up' before then, and a new era (The Millennial Age) will begin.

Now, there will be no power here to prevent the Beast from executing his plan, for this is the will of God. Humanity will be living in an era that far surpasses all others regarding destruction and excruciating suffering. However, a few will escape the onslaught and destruction. The Beast will attempt to establish his domain by promoting his brand, the mark of the Beast (666), which is the mark of a man. His endeavor is to encourage everyone to receive the mark, bow down, and worship the Beast. Whoever does not bow down and worship or accept the mark of the beast will be executed. This is not to intimidate anyone but to remind us of what lies ahead for those left behind after the rapture.

And I beheld another beast coming up out of the earth; and he had
two horns like a lamb, and he spake as a dragon. And he exerciseth
all the power of the first beast before him, and causeth the earth and

them which dwell therein to worship the first beast, whose deadly wound was healed. And he doeth great wonders, so that he maketh fire come down from heaven on the earth in the sight of men, and deceiveth them that dwell on the earth by the means of those miracles which he had power to do in the sight of the beast; saying to them that dwell on the earth, that they should make an image to the beast, which had the wound by a sword and did live. And he had power to give life unto the image of the beast, that the image of the beast should both speak, and cause that as many as would not worship the image of the beast should be killed.

And he causeth all, both small and great, rich and poor, free and bond, to receive a mark in their right hand, or in their foreheads: and that no man might buy or sell, save he that had the mark, or the name of the beast, or the number of his name. Here is wisdom. Let him that hath understanding count the number of the beast: for it is the number of a man; and his number is Six hundred threescore and six.

REVELATION 13:11-18

Those who refuse the mark and are faithful to death may have a chance at the first resurrection. In that phase of human life, an individual has two options: they can either refuse the mark and be killed or accept it and perish forever. Again, the church will be nowhere around here. The Antichrist will demonstrate his power then, deceiving many who refuse God's knowledge and the things concerning Him. There is a way to escape the beast and his mark: to accept Jesus Christ today as Lord and Savior of your life. Tomorrow is a promise to no one. If you read this book and have not accepted Jesus, do it now. Our Heavenly Father will not wait when it's time to execute his will. Each one of us were allotted enough time here on earth to seek Him so that we can be saved from the terror that is to come. Living in this life now is even more challenging than when we first started as babies and toddlers. Time has changed drastically for the better for some of us and others, the worse. Nevertheless, God still calls out, saying, "Look this way, I Am the solution."

To overcome the beasts that cause frustration in our lives, we must abide in Christ. Run away all you can; through the valley, down the steep hill, over the mountain, and bypassing the desert, you will still run right into Him! Jesus is the answer and the only way out. No one will escape. Someone might think, "It's hard to live as a child of God, or I don't like too many rules." Now think about it: wouldn't you think a child would rather listen to their parents than a bully? Often, a parent would instruct you out of love; "don't do this, do that, don't go over there, walk this way," etc. On the other hand, a bully doesn't care who you are, much less to be concerned about your well-being. A bully would shove you around, mistreat and abuse you, beat you down, and run you over.

Not accepting God's tender love and affection sets oneself up for permanent failure. The bible suggested that His commandments are not grievous. The only option left is being handed over to the bully, which is the devil and his agents. Now let me remind you that there is nothing called love where the devil and his angels' abode. Another name for hell is everlasting punishment, which is greater than death. Don't worry about death, for when an individual dies, it's just an expiration of the components they are made up of. What belongs to the natural world (your dust-like bodily form) returns to its original place. What belongs to the spiritual world (your inward man) goes back to the spirit world. However, the soul lives on, waiting to be released and clothed with a new body. Thus, that body will be determined according to where you are headed- Heaven or Hell.

To have gone through hell on earth (spiritual and physical pain and suffering) and to face an eternal hell is a life of futility and worthlessness. It wouldn't make sense to be in existence after all, would it? Humans came into existence for a reason: to serve, worship, and honor the Great I Am, the God who made heaven and earth. Nothing else. Our very existence is not for us. We could not call ourselves into being or into existence, for that matter. This knowledge and intelligence tell us that we have a Superior above us. That's a God to whom we owe everything- even the breath we breathe. Do we see the picture now? None of us can turn a single strand of our hair black or white. When Mr. Gray shows up, we could dye as much as we like, but our hair will return to the former state it was before. This is one aspect of life that tells us that we are not in control here. Thus, it is one reason we should acknowledge God and what He requires of us.

Man, who was made with the highest level of intelligence, sometimes doesn't have a sense of direction. The enemy fills the gap when we fail to seek God and include Him in our lives. Now, having no power, ability, or preeminence (without God), the adversary will soon swallow us up quickly. My friend, do you see how important it is to have God in our lives? No child being pushed out of the womb grows up automatically. As it is in the natural birth, so is it in the spiritual. When we come to Christ, we experience a spiritual birth, and from there on, we gradually grow into spiritual maturity. God is not demanding that we grow up and be mature immediately. He orchestrated it so that as we grow, we gain knowledge and understanding, which is wisdom. However, we cannot attempt this all by ourselves, but He assists us all the way.

God, the Creator of the universe and Earth's rightful owner, knew that all these things we are facing in this world would happen. We should never think for one minute that He had lost control of the wheel. Everything is going perfectly as he planned. How do we know? It's because everything that everyone else planned (including the devil), contrary to His will, never last! From the beginning, the sun planted in the skies (approximately 92,960,000 miles from the Earth) never ceased to shine or even be exhausted. The skies or the heavens are still where they were from the beginning. All that God had put in place, nothing seems to fail but humans. This is the result of evil influence from outsiders. The Devil started a fire in Heaven, knowing not that the Greater fire would prevail. Now, he and his bandit intend to finish what they have begun in heaven. Thus, they are using willing and vulnerable victims to execute their will.

Thus, knowing all these things, God cannot be instructed by anyone. The Master of the universe does whatever pleases Him. So, whatever He allows, it is for His pleasure. Although He is the invisible God, He requires humanity to know and understand His ways so that we can please Him. God's intention towards humanity doesn't change. He made humanity so they could coexist with Him. God gave us choices; we can decide to live with him, or we can choose to go the other way. In other words, we called the shots based on our decisions.

> *For God so loved the world, that he gave his only begotten Son, that whosoever believeth in Him should not perish, but have everlasting life.*

JOHN 3:16

Jesus had sacrificed His life for us. The Devil thought He won, but Jesus overcame by paying Hell a visit (snatched the keys of Hell and Death), rose Himself up on the third day, ran a few errands on Earth, and then ascended into Heaven as the King of Glory. That was a heavy blow to the Devil and another fulfillment of the word of God.

> *And I will put enmity between thee and the woman, and between thy seed and her seed; it shall bruise thy head, and thou shalt bruise his heel.*

GENESIS 3:15

The Devil was defeated at Calvary when Jesus gave up the Ghost and said, 'it is finished.' Satan didn't have a clue what was taking place. He was led into an ambush and an entrapment! Now, he's being defeated forever. Jesus opened the way for whoever received Him and accepted this full and free salvation would eventually be saved.

CHAPTER 14
UNLEASHING SPIRITUAL AUTHORITY

M any in Christendom today live a life of defeat simply because they fail to execute the authority given to them through the blood of Jesus Christ. In our journey as faith warriors, a realm exists beyond the tangible, a domain where spiritual authority reigns supreme. This chapter delves into the profound concept of unleashing spiritual authority and how it empowers the children of God to launch a relentless onslaught on the enemy. Spiritual authority is not merely a theoretical concept or reasoning that is ineffective when applicable, but a tangible reality within the Christian faith-walk with their God. It emanates from the divine relationship between God and His children. It is a power granted to believers through their connection with the Almighty, enabling them to operate in the supernatural realm. This authority is not dependent on worldly credentials or human prowess but is bestowed upon every believer through the indwelling of the Holy
Spirit.

The source of spiritual authority lies in the redemptive work of Jesus Christ. Through His death and resurrection, Jesus defeated the powers of darkness and reclaimed authority over all realms. Believers inherit spiritual authority as heirs of this victory, becoming ambassadors of Christ on earth. This authority is not rooted in personal merit but in the grace and righteousness of Christ. Jesus told His disciples while he was with them on earth that He had given them power over all the power of the enemy and that nothing shall by any means harm them. Now, my friend, can you start to imagine the magnitude of this authority God has given man? Do you remember what the Book of Genesis suggested about the authority God had given to humanity when he carved him in His image and likeness? However, as we know, man lost that authority when He failed to obey God in the Garden of Eden. Ever since then, all that surrounds him is chaos and violence. Sin has caused the enemy to access and corrupt everything associated with man.

Now, when Jesus came (who is the second Adam), He restored everything that man had ever lost- even his God-given authority and identity. Human has access to complete freedom (through the efficacious blood of Jesus Christ, the sacrificial lamb) from the chains and bondage that sin had caused. Thus, Man was restored to his former status as the son of God. However, we would have to face a fierce battle against the adversary of our souls trying to prevent us from inheriting the kingdom. However, spiritual authority cannot be effective without the execution of faith. When faith is executed, things happen in the spiritual and physical realms. The exceptional connection or relationship between a remote mechanism and a remote-control device caused both to function effectively. So it is, with faith and Almighty God. Not in the sense that God is some robotic mechanism. However, we cannot get or achieve anything from God without faith. God operates in the intangible realm of invisibility and consciousness. "Why would God operate thus?" One would ask. Well - He is God and not merely human. He is not made, created, or formed; He is self-existent: He cannot change. Thus, the only way to unlock our spiritual authority is through faith, which allows us to access the power and blessings of God.

To unleash spiritual authority, believers must first acknowledge their identity as children of God. In other words, we must first know who we are and whom we belong. We are not powerless spectators in the cosmic battle, but active participants armed with divine authority to wage war against principalities and opposing powers. To be victorious and triumphant against the ruler of darkness, sons of God must first align themselves to God's will and purpose. With constant fasting and prayer, studying and exercising the word of God, we, as God's children, can dismantle and bring to naught every stronghold of the adversary. Unleashing spiritual authority can cause significant damage to the kingdom of darkness. Those willing to fight often find themselves without support or assistance from their fellow brethren.

Notwithstanding, we are still striving towards perfection, but while we are thriving, we should be watching each other back. No military force ever won a battle without being in unison. God told Israel that as long as they obeyed His will and commandments, no one could stand before or against them. He also assured them that one man shall chase a thousand enemies, and two shall chase ten thousand! Unity among believers is not just crucial for ultimate victory; it is our strength to drive back the enemy into a far place. It strengthens our collective spiritual authority and makes us more effective in our battle against the adversary. It fosters a sense of camaraderie and collective strength, reminding us that we are not alone in this fight.

Satan and his demonic forces seek to thwart God's plans and oppress humanity. However, believers armed with spiritual authority can confront and overcome the enemy. Through prayer, fasting, and the proclamation of God's Word, we can launch a powerful onslaught on the forces of darkness. By standing firm in faith and wielding our spiritual weapons, believers enforce God's victory and dismantle the enemy's strongholds. This is not a vain battle or one we are fighting alone, but one where we are assured victory. It is a reassurance that should fill us with confidence and strengthen our resolve.

Unleashing spiritual authority is not a mere theoretical concept but a transformative reality for believers. It is one where we stand on the authority of God, wage spiritual war against principalities and powers, overcome obstacles, walk in the victory that follows, and impact the world. As children of God, empowered by the Holy Spirit, believers have the authority to launch an unyielding onslaught on the enemy's schemes. By embracing their identity and standing firm in faith, they usher in the manifestation of God's kingdom on earth. Duty's call beckons believers to rise in spiritual authority and fulfill their divine mandate. Consistency is the secret to having victory repeatedly by simple faith and obedience. Though we use this cliche:

"No one is perfect" countless times, we must admit that good practice makes one perfect. An athlete running a race makes certain they practice frequently and sometimes to the extreme to achieve their goals. And so it is, with a child of God. Prayer, fasting, studying God's word, and living righteously can cause considerable damage to the kingdom of darkness.

If we want to see devils and demons scrambling, we must wear God's armor. Too many courageous individuals are walking around as if their captain is weak. The Holy Ghost or the Comforter Jesus promised to send, is God living inside us. The Holy Ghost never sleeps, never becomes weak, or has any form of infirmity whatsoever. He is God in man. So now that we know what is inside of us, let us 'quit ye like men and be strong'! [1 Corinthians 16:13].

Many Christians do not understand the art of spiritual warfare. Thus, we do not know how to fight, so we lose many authoritative battles. A spiritual boot camp is necessary for a child of God to ride the rough and choppy waves that the world and the enemy occasionally throw at us. We must learn how to master effective prayer, fasting, and the study of God's word. In other words, we are warriors of the cross!

Thou, therefore, my son, be strong in the grace that is in Christ Jesus. And the things that thou hast heard of me among many witnesses, the same commit to faithful men, who shall be able to teach others also. Thou, therefore, endure hardness, as a good soldier of Jesus Christ. No man that warreth entangleth himself with the affairs of this life; that he may please him who hath chosen him to be a soldier.

2 TIMOTHY 2: 1-4

To take this Christian pathway lightly is like sticking one's hand in a viper's hole and expecting nothing to happen! Such a thought would be self-delusional. Taking up one's cross and following Jesus Christ daily is a sacrifice. The spiritual journey will not be easy at times. The enemy will launch all sorts of artillery our way. Thus, it is essential to be fully armored. This kind of warfare is critical. We cannot fight it alone. Many tried and are still trying and failed miserably. Having God walking with you in this world that lies in wickedness is paramount. The whole earth has become a minefield. Without God, we cannot see where we are headed. That tells us that we must trust in Him completely.

The psalmist declares:

> *If it had not been the Lord who was on our side, now may Israel say; If it had not been the Lord who was on our side when men rose up against us: Then they had swallowed us up quick, when their wrath was kindled against us: Then the waters had overwhelmed us, the stream had gone over our soul: Then the proud waters had gone over our soul: Blessed be the name of the Lord, who hath not given us as a prey to their teeth. Our soul is escaped as a bird out of the snare of the fowlers: the snare is broken and we are escaped. Our help is in the name of the Lord, who made heaven and earth.*

PSALM 124

To underestimate our captain's commands and strategy to wage war against the adversary can bring complete failure or disaster. We must understand that our warfare is not against flesh and blood. Therefore, it is utterly useless to carry knives, guns, bombs, and machetes against an individual we think is our enemy. There is a real culprit behind all the chaos and melee- and that is Satan. Unless we obtain spiritual intelligence to know how to fight, we will constantly be failing. We must pray and ask God for direction when a particular issue appears. Next, we must follow His specific instructions.

Most children of God become defeated in spiritual battles because they fail to follow God's instructions. Sometimes, these instructions may seem illogical or unreasonable in grave circumstances, but victory is inevitable if we do as He says. "How often do we see God using foolish things to defeat and confound the enemy? Would God dare to use anything at all? Can He use a rod, a donkey, a stone, and a sling? Or can He use instruments, songs, and music?" Well, be assured that He can!

Let's take a look at what happened in the days of King Jehoshaphat when there was a threat from the enemy of God's people:

> *Then upon Jahaziel the son of Zechariah, the son of Benaiah, the son of Jeiel, the son of Mattaniah, a Levite of the sons of Asaph, came the Spirit of the Lord in the midst of the congregation; And he said, Hearken ye all Judah, and ye inhabitants of Jerusalem, and thou king Jehoshaphat, Thus saith the Lord unto you, Be not afraid or dismayed by reason of this great multitude; for the battle is not your's but God's. Tomorrow go ye down against them: behold they come up by the cliff of Ziz; and ye shall find them at the end of the brook, before the wilderness of Jeruel. Ye shall not need to fight in this battle: set yourselves, stand ye still, and see the salvation of the Lord with you, O Jerusalem: fear not, nor be dismayed; to morrow go out against them: for the Lord will be with you.*

> *And Jehoshaphat bowed his head with his face to the ground: and all Judah and the inhabitants of Jerusalem fell before the Lord, worshipping the Lord. And the Levites of the children of the Kohathites and of the children of Korhites stood up to praise the Lord God of Israel with a loud voice on high. And they rose early in the morning and went forth into the wilderness of Tekoa: and as they went forth, Jehoshaphat stood and said, hear me O Judah and ye inhabitants of Jerusalem; Believe in the Lord your God, so shall ye be established; believe His prophets, so shall ye prosper. And when he had consulted with the people, he appointed singers unto the Lord, and that they should praise the beauty of holiness, as they went out before the army, and to say Praise the Lord; for His mercy endureth forever. And when they began to sing and to praise, the Lord set ambushments against the children of Ammon, Moab, and Mount Seir, which were come against Judah, and they were smitten.*

For the children of Ammon and Moab stood up against the inhabitants
of mount Seir utterly to slay and to destroy them. And when they had
made an end of the inhabitants of Seir, everyone helped to destroy
another. And Judah came toward the watch tower in the wilderness,
they looked unto the multitude and behold they were dead bodies fallen
to the earth and none escaped. And when Jehoshaphat and his people
came to take away the spoil of them, they found among them in
abundance both riches with the dead bodies, and precious jewels, which
they stripped off for themselves, more than they could carry away: and
they were three days in gathering the spoil, it was so much.

2 CHRONICLES 20: 14-25

Trusting and obeying God's instructions is imperative to unleash our spiritual authority. However, our lifestyle must be conducive to His word and ordinances. When touching God's spiritual things, "attention to details is paramount. Obeying His instructions is honoring Him. Let us always seek to honor God. When we honor God, He will always honor our requests. When we call on His name, He will come to us quickly. Many individuals only call on God when they are in trouble. However, we must be like the Psalmist and utter:

I will bless the LORD at all times: His praise shall continually be in
my mouth. My soul shall make her boast in the LORD: the humble
shall hear thereof, and be glad.

PSALM 34:1-2

It is impossible to unleash our spiritual authority when our spiritual life is hindered. Sin, for example, is one reason we don't normally see results when launching a counterattack against the enemy. Sometimes, there is a hindered channel that needs to be rectified. As soon as we find and address the issue, we'll return to winning streaks to the honor and the glory of Almighty God. It is a great feeling to rejoice in the LORD., especially when He has caused you to overcome the onslaught of the wicked. Some people won't give God the glory because they think there is no reason to. It makes one want to believe, how is it that they are still alive and breathing? No one would still be standing today without God being merciful to us:

If it had not been the LORD who was on our side, when men rose up against us: Then they had swallowed us up quick.

PSALM 124: 2-3

Living without God in these trying times is risky. This is because an individual would become a prime target for the enemy. In other words, the adversary could easily slap them around like a helpless creature. On the other hand, a child of God would be more than equipped to deter the onslaught and put the adversary under subjection. Do you see how imperative it is to have the Holy Ghost with power operating in our lives? The Scripture suggested that when the enemy comes in like a flood, the Spirit of God will lift up a standard against him. [Isaiah 59:19]

We are never alone in a spiritual battle as long as we stay in Christ Jesus. God's grace and mercy will keep you through the fire, flood, and even great troubles and trials. During my spiritual battle back home in Jamaica, I didn't see an ending to the ongoing attack by these demonic forces from night to night. This was my first time being engaged in spiritual warfare, so I didn't know how things would have worked out. Nevertheless, I decided not to lie down and die. With each attack, every night, I was singing, clapping, shouting, praying, and giving God the glory. Moreover, each night, I realized I had won (nobody else had died or fallen ill); I grew stronger spiritually! Although I felt a bit exhausted by the end of the week, God stepped in right on time and gave us the victory!

Watching God fighting for us and giving us total victory is phenomenal. The rest is history- for if He did it already, He will do it again and again. Many more battles will come after the first, but at least we will remember the former victory and be confident that these also will be won through Jesus

Christ. Fighting a spiritual battle with a carnal weapon would be a total loss. We must fight the way God commands us to. Many times, children of God endeavor to take on a particular situation in their own way. Our way will always be carnal, but if we fight our battle God's way, we will come out victorious. The carnal mind always gets in the way and always wants to hurt or offend somebody. Many times, we wound up harming our own selves. No wonder the second greatest command that God gave His people is to 'love our neighbors (another human being) as ourselves.'

> *But when the Pharisees had heard that He had put the Sadducees to silence, they were gathered together. Then one of them, who was a lawyer, asked him a question, tempting him and saying, Master, which is the great commandment in the law? Jesus said unto him, Thou shalt love the Lord thy God with all thy heart, and with all thy soul, and with all thy mind. This is the first and great commandment. And the second is like unto it, Thou shalt love thy neighbor as thyself. On these two commandments hang all the law and the prophets.*
>
> MATTHEW 22:34-40

There is no place for hatred in the kingdom of God; that kind of emotion and trait belongs to the devil. Our spiritual authority will be hindered when there are bits and pieces of traits of the enemy lingering in our lives. Often, children of God failed miserably and wondered why. Cain eventually became a murderer because he failed and further refused to correct the spiritual blunder in his life. Thus, instead of executing his God-given spiritual authority, he was consumed by the Wicked One. We must prioritize breaking off every negative trait and habit that prevents us from unleashing our spiritual authority and reaching our full potential in God. There is only one Master of the universe, and His name is Jesus. All resources come from Him. Nothing can function without Almighty God. Humans were given the authority to reign on earth until they lost it through disobedience. Jesus came and restored all that we have lost. Now we have power over all the devil's power through Jesus Christ our LORD. Sadly, many still haven't woken up to this fact.

Before Christ came, the adversary of our souls would oppress us daily. There was no rest. We were bound spiritually with chains and fetters. Yes, my friend, there was no hope for humanity, but thanks be to the Lamb that was slain before the foundation of the world.

> *Forasmuch as ye know that ye were not redeemed with corruptible things, as silver and gold, from your vain conversation received by tradition from your fathers; but with the precious blood of Christ, as of a lamb without blemish and without spot: who verily was foreordained before the foundation of the world, but was manifest in these last times for you, who by him do believe in God, that raised him up from the dead, and gave him glory; that your faith and hope may be in God.*

> 1 PETER1:18-21

Sadly, many will remain in their former state because they refuse to change. There is no escape for neglecting or even rejecting the gospel. Rejecting means no victory and no abundant life. Some folks will remain miserable all the days of their lives because of the choice of not accepting this full and free salvation. Their heart became hardened, and so they pine away slowly and quietly. They often stumble and fall but do not know why or what they stumbled at. Instead of having God-given authority, they are under heavy burden. This is precisely what God said would happen to His people, Israel, if they disobey and refuse to do His will!

As I write, is it a coincidence that this is happening to all nations now? Of course not. God's law and ordinances have been around since Jacob's (Israel) children left the land of bondage and headed for the promised land. God gave them His law through Moses and also the consequences of not keeping the same:

But unto them that are contentious, and do not obey the truth, but obey unrighteousness, indignation, and wrath, tribulation, and anguish, upon every soul of man that doeth evil, of the Jew first, and also of the Gentile; for there is no respect of persons with God.

ROMANS 2:8-11

CHAPTER 15
VICTORIOUS LIVING

Have you ever encountered someone so overwhelmed with life's issues that when you start a conversation, that person begins to pour out? Yes, it's real, my friend. Moreover, often, your situation cannot be compared to what this individual might be going through and vice versa. However, as humans, we all have one common ground: the different issues we face in life. How we approach these issues and solve them is very important. You can either choose to be victorious or writhe in pain and resentment (all the days of your life) because of that curved ball that deceptively spun and smashed you right in the face! A soldier with a purple heart is still a soldier. Over the years, he may still have some signs of being wounded, but the essence is that he had been to war. As soldiers of the cross and warriors for a cause, let us look into ways to start living victoriously for God.

Firstly, we can never conquer life's issues alone. Attempting to take on life's problems alone is like going on a suicide mission! "Why is that so?" because there are dark entities that will stop at nothing to try and defeat our purposes. As an individual ventures alone on this path to end their problems, that person soon finds out that it wouldn't be all that easy. The pressure on the mind brings about stress. Then, that stress moves into another phase called distress. Then distress becomes oppression. Oppression then moves to the stage called depression. Finally, the individual flung open a door that invites the spirit of possession, and we know what happened next- The result often led to mental instability and usually insanity. Not only that, but suicidal thoughts started kicking in also. Therefore, we need help to take on life's challenges from a power much greater than the ones opposing us, and that is my friend, Almighty God.

Living a victorious life can seem like a distant dream for many in a world filled with challenges and strife. However, for those who identify as children of God, victorious living is not just a lofty ideal, but a tangible reality promised in Scripture. On that note, we will explore what it means to be a child of God, living daily in constant victory. Victorious living goes far beyond what this world may perceive as mere success or prosperity. A true victorious living must be seen from a spiritual point of view. It encompasses peace, joy, and contentment even amid life's storms. It's about overcoming sin, conquering fear, and triumphing over adversity through the power and presence of God in one's life. But what does it mean to live victoriously, and how does this concept intertwine with the identity of being a child of God? Through biblical insights, practical advice, and personal reflections, we will uncover the essence of victorious living and how it manifests in the life of a believer. This victory is not confined to the spiritual realm but extends to every aspect of a believer's life, including personal struggles, societal pressures, and the universal quest for meaning.

The Bible is replete with instances of victorious living, from the faith of Abraham, who

against all hope, believed and so became the father of many nations

ROMANS 4:18

to the steadfastness of Paul, who declared,

I have fought the good fight, I have finished the race, I have kept the faith.

2 TIMOTHY 4:7

These examples highlight that victory is not the absence of problems but the presence of divine strength and perseverance. Central to experiencing victorious living is the role of faith and the Holy Spirit. Faith is the foundation upon which believers stand, facing life's challenges with great confidence in God's promises. The Holy Spirit, on the other hand, empowers and guides us, cultivating within us the strength, wisdom, and grace needed to overcome.

The journey of victorious living begins with understanding our fundamental identity as children of God. This identity is not earned through deeds or merits but is a gift of grace through faith in Jesus Christ. When we are baptized in Jesus's name and receive the gift of the Holy Ghost (the spirit of adoption), we automatically become sons of God:

> *But as many as received him, to them gave him power to become sons of God, ...*

> JOHN 1:12

This adoption into God's family marks the start of a transformative journey, reshaping our self-perception, values, and purpose. Being a child of God means our identity is anchored in Christ. This profound truth influences how we view ourselves and our circumstances. Instead of defining our worth by worldly standards or past failures, we recognize ourselves as redeemed, loved, and empowered by God. This new identity is the bedrock of victorious living, aligning our thoughts, actions, and desires with God's will. One of the most remarkable aspects of this identity is its transformative power. As we grow in our relationship with God, our character begins to reflect His character. This internal transformation affects our heart and spirit, and external influences our behavior and interactions.

The evidence of a child of God is seen in the fruit of the Spirit, which Galatians 5:22-23 describes as 'love, joy, peace, longsuffering, gentleness, goodness, faith, meekness, temperance.' These attributes are not mere moral virtues but the natural outcomes of the Holy Spirit's work within us. They signify a life increasingly victorious over the flesh and aligned with the divine nature. What awesomeness is that! Each aspect of the fruit of the Spirit contributes to victorious living. Love empowers us to overcome selfishness and serve others selflessly. Joy allows us to find contentment and happiness in God, even in grave and tumultuous trials. Peace anchors our hearts in the assurance of God's sovereignty, irrespective of external chaos. As children of the most high God, our pursuit of victorious living is not a solitary endeavor, but a collective journey shared with fellow believers. The transformation we experience as individuals has a ripple effect, influencing our families, communities, and the broader world. Living victoriously, as described in the lives of those who are children of God, is not merely theoretical but intensely practical. It involves daily habits, choices, and commitments that align with our identity in Christ and empower us to live out our divine calling.

There are practical steps believers can take to cultivate a lifestyle of victory by focusing on daily spiritual disciplines, the importance of community, and the power of service and witnessing.

Victorious living requires intentionality and discipline. While our victory is ultimately secured in Christ, experiencing it daily involves engaging in practices that draw us closer to God and align our lives with His purposes. Some vital practices foster a lifestyle of victory, such as constant prayer, studying the Word, and fasting. Prayer is our direct line of communication with God, a means to express our gratitude, seek guidance, and intercede for others. In these moments of prayer, we often find the strength to overcome our challenges.

Similarly, the Word of God is described as a *lamp to*

our feet and a light to our path

PSALM 119:105

Scriptures instruct us in righteousness and provide comfort, conviction, and wisdom. Regular engagement with the Bible shapes our worldview, guides our decisions, and reinforces our identity in Christ. Moreover, practicing or living out the word of God can have an incredible impact on the lives of the saints of God and others around them. The Christian faith was never meant to be lived in isolation. Victorious living thrives in the context of community and fellowship with other believers. The early church modeled this through communal prayer, worship, and resource-sharing (Acts 2:42-47). Today, being part of a faith community provides accountability, support, and encouragement. In these gatherings, we are reminded of God's faithfulness, our challenge to grow, and to be equipped to serve others.

Engagement in small groups, Bible study meetings, or church ministries deepens our spiritual life and connects us with others who can walk with us in our journey toward victory. With a decision to equip ourselves with the arsenals given to us by God through faith and with the power of the Holy Ghost, we can overcome any trials or even temptations. Jesus warned that we would have trouble in this life but reminded us to take heart because He has overcome the world (John 16:33). Overcoming trials and temptations is a mark of victorious living. Faith is our crucial weapon in this battle. Faith in God's promises and faithfulness enables us to face challenges with courage and perseverance. Through these experiences, our faith is refined, our character is built, and our dependency on God is deepened. Now, living victoriously is evidenced by our love and services to others. Jesus set the ultimate example of service, and as His followers, we are called to do the same. Serving others, whether through acts of kindness, volunteering, or spiritual mentorship, reflects the heart of God to the world. Moreover, victorious living compels us to share our hope in Christ. Witnessing to others, whether through personal testimony, sharing the gospel, or living out our faith authentically, will eventually draw others to the victory we have in Jesus.

Victorious living does more than transform individual lives; it influences relationships, shapes communities, and serves as a beacon of hope and light in a world that often seems dominated by darkness. As we conclude our journey through the concept of victorious living and its correlation with the lifestyle of a child of God, it's clear that this is not merely an ideal to aspire to but a reality to be experienced. Living victoriously is rooted in our identity in Christ, empowered by the Holy Spirit, and manifested through our daily lives. It is a testimony to God's grace, a source of hope and inspiration to others, and a powerful force for good in the world. We are called to live victoriously, not in our strength, but in the power of the One who has overcome the world, Jesus Christ of Nazareth. May we embrace this calling with faith and courage, knowing that, in Christ, we are more than conquerors. Let us pursue victorious living with determination and joy, for in doing so, we fulfill our highest calling as children of God.

The promise that God gave us is not for the afterlife only. Jesus told His disciples that He came to provide us with life and that more abundantly! "Now, what does this mean?" someone may ask. The abundant life is simply the freedom we have in Christ to prosper. God told the children of Israel that if they would trust and obey Him, specific blessings would automatically overtake them. Thus, that promise of abundant life automatically transferred from the Old Testament and spilled over into the new!

> And it shall come to pass, if thou shalt hearken diligently unto the voice of the LORD thy God, to observe and to do all His commandments which I command thee this day, that the Lord thy God will set thee on high above all nations of the earth: and all these blessings shall come on thee, and overtake thee, if thou shalt hearken unto the voice of the LORD thy God. Blessed shalt thou be in the city, and blessed shalt thou be in the field:

> Blessed shalt be the fruit of thy body, and the fruit of thy ground, and the fruit of thy cattle, the increase of thy kine, and the flocks of thy sheep. Blessed shall be thy basket and thy store. Blessed shalt thou be when thou comest in, and blessed shalt thou be when thou goest out. The LORD shall cause thine enemies that rise up against thee

to be smitten before thy face: they shall come out against thee one way and flee before thee seven ways. The LORD shall command the blessing upon thee in thy storehouses, and in all that thou settest thine hand unto: and he shall bless thee in the land which the LORD thy God giveth thee. The LORD shall establish thee an holy people unto Himself, as He hath sworn unto thee, if thou shalt keep the commandments of the LORD thy God, and walk in His ways.

And all the people of the earth shall see that thou art called by the name of the LORD; and they shall be afraid of thee. And the Lord shall make thee plenteous in goods, in the fruit of thy body, and in the fruit of thy cattle, and in the fruit of thy ground, and in the land which the LORD sware unto thy fathers to give thee. The LORD shall open unto thee His good treasure, the heaven to give the rain unto thy land in his season, and to bless all the work of thine hand: and thou shalt lend unto many nations, and thou shalt not borrow. And the LORD shall make thee the head and not the tail; and thou shalt be above only, and thou shalt not be beneath; if thou hearken unto the commandments of the LORD thy God, which I commanded thee this day, to observe and to do them.

DEUTERONOMY 28: 1-13

So, my friend, we see that the promise from way back then fell on the church of Jesus Christ! What a mighty God we serve!

A light bulb went off in the core of Peter's being when he went to minister to the gentile man Cornelius (A Gentile) and his household. Now up to this point in time, the Gentiles (sinners or unbelievers) had not been exposed to the gospel. However, God was about to burst the door wide open for whoever will. Peter was lodging at Joppa with one Simon a tanner when he had a vision while praying on the rooftop. In the vision, Peter saw a vessel descending from above filled with all kinds of unclean animals and heard the voice of the Lord instructing him to rise, kill, and eat. Now, according to the law given to Moses by God, there are certain animals, including birds, that an Israelite is forbidden to eat. So, when this vessel descended, Peter heard the voice say kill and eat, and his response was no, "Why?" Because, as an Israelite, he knew what the Judaic law entails. This happened thrice (with Peter reiterating) before the vessel finally disappeared.

As Peter was pondering over the vision and what it meant, three men came looking for him from Cornelius' house:

And they said, Cornelius the centurion, a just man, and one that feareth God, and of good report among all the nation of the Jews, was warned from God by an holy angel to send for thee into his house, and to hear words of thee. Then called he them in, and lodged them. And on the morrow Peter went away with them, and certain brethren from Joppa accompanied him;

On the morrow after they entered into Caesarea. And Cornelius waited for them, and and had called together his kinsmen and near friends. And as Peter was coming in, Cornelius met him, and fell down at his feet, and worshipped him. But Peter took him up, saying stand up; I myself also am a man. And as he talked with him, he went in, and found many that were come together. And he said unto them, Ye know how that it is an unlawful thing for a man that is a Jew to keep company, or come unto one of another nation; but God hath shewed me that I should not call any man common or unclean. Therefore came I unto you without gainsaying, as soon as I was sent for: I ask therefore for what intent ye have sent for me?

And Cornelius said, four days ago I was fasting until this hour; and at the ninth hour I prayed in my house, and behold a man stood before me in bright clothing, and said, Cornelius, thy prayer is heard and thy alms are had in rememberance in the sight of God. Send therefore to Joppa, and call hither Simon, whose surname is Peter; he lodged in the house of one Simon a tanner by the sea side: who, when he cometh, shall speak unto thee. Immediately therefore I sent to thee; and thou hast well done that thou art come. Now, therefore, are we all here present before God, to hear all things that are commanded thee of God. Then Peter opened his mouth, and said, of a truth I perceived that God is no respector of persons: but in every nation he that feareth him, and worketh righteousness, is accepted with him.

ACTS 10:30-35

Victorious living is for those willing to acknowledge that there is one unique God over all the universe and to fear the same by doing righteously. Many people desire to live joyfully and unperturbed from their fellow humans or any other kind of interference. Unfortunately, life doesn't work like that. Since the fall of Adam, heartache, pain, long-suffering, distress, and hopelessness have plagued man's life until Jesus Christ of Nazareth appeared on the scene. Jesus came to give us hope and to restore us from our fallen state. Furthermore, He came to provide us with life, and that more abundantly!

Abundant life is victorious living. This can only be found in Jesus. If we receive Him, we will attain it; if we do not, our whole life will be in misery. The awesomeness of God surpassed all understandings of humanity. Though the entire world may seem to be in turmoil, He gives grace and peace to His beloved. The grace He placed on us caused unbelievers to wonder why we are so different from everyone else. At our spiritual birth, the supernatural power of Almighty God caused a spiritual separation. Thus, we are in the world (physically), but we are no longer attached to the same-spiritually speaking. When Jesus was about to be given up to be crucified, He prayed for His disciples in this manner:

> *While I was with them in the world, I kept them in thy name: those that thou gavest me I have kept, and none of them are lost, but the son of perdition; that the scripture might be fulfilled.*

> *And now come I to thee; and these things I speak in the world, that they might have my joy fulfilled in themselves. I have given them thy word, and the world hath hated them because they are not of the world, even as I am not of the world. I pray not that thou shouldest take them out of the world, but that thou shouldest keep them from evil. They are not of the world, even as I am not of the world.*

JOHN 17:12-16

When we are baptized in Jesus's name and filled with the Holy Ghost, we are automatically ushered into the kingdom- old things are passed away, and all things become new. We no longer have the mind of the world, but we strive always to have the mind of Christ. The moment we get it right, there is no telling the joy and peace that will overflow in our lives! This is what Jesus promised from the beginning! This is victorious living! Only those who have experienced God can attest to it. The scriptures encourage us to taste and see that the LORD is good; the man who trusts in Him shall be blessed. Have you accepted Jesus as your LORD and Savior? Or are you wasting time looking for other solutions for your troubles? Time is running out, and soon, you may desire to seek him, but it might be too late. If you are that one, please don't delay; receive Him gladly while you have the opportunity.

It is impossible for a child of God to live a life of defeat when donned in His righteousness.

> Then they that feared the LORD spake often one to another: and the Lord hearkened, and heard it, and a book of rememberance was written before him for them that feared the LORD, and thought upon His name. And they shall be mine, saith the LORD of hosts, in that day when I make up my jewels; and I will spare them, as a man spareth his own son that serveth him. Then shall ye return, and discern between the righteous and the wicked, between him that serveth God and him that serveth him not.

> MALACHI 3:16-18

God promised us a victorious lifestyle when we came to Him. He told the children of Israel that no weapon formed against them shall prosper, and every tongue that rises against them in judgment shall be condemned. Interfering with or coming against God's people is a grave matter to Him. No one will escape this judgment. Sooner or later, someone will be punished for coming against His beloved:

After the glory hath he sent me unto the nations which spoiled you: for him that toucheth you toucheth the apple of his eye.

ZECHARIAH 2:7-8

God will eventually rid Himself of those who tried to destroy His people. Ultimate destruction will come to those who refuse to repent and turn from their wicked ways. There is no hope or solution for the prideful individuals who scoffed at God's people and His word. Everyone will be judged according to their works or deeds.

CHAPTER 16

EXPERIENCE WORTH LIVING FOR

In the Book of Ecclesiastes, Solomon, the son of David, made many wise observations that still resonate with the lives of many individuals today. One profound observation is found in Ecclesiastes 6:3, which states thus:

If a man beget an hundred children, and live many years, so that the days of his years be many, and his soul be not filled with good, and also that he had no burial; I say that an untimely death is better than he.

Wow, that's a mouthful from the wisest man ever lived! But when you come to think of it, it does make a whole lot of sense. Imagine an individual spending their entire life trying to achieve and excel to the highest level possible- but at the end of the day, they didn't live their life to the fullest. Moreover, without time for laughter, joy, or meaningful fulfillment, life wouldn't make any sense whatsoever.

When God placed man on earth, He had one thing in mind- to make him feel very happy about his existence and enjoy all He has to offer. However, man encountered the worst nightmare of his life (which is the devil) that caused things to go downward in a spiral direction. Yes, my friend, whatever you may be going through right now, life wasn't meant to be like that. However, there is hope in God for all that we have l lost.

He promises to restore all-even our very soul! Hallelujah! What an awesome God!

For those of you reading this book right now who have not yet encountered God in your life, now is the time. You may wonder why I sometimes become emotional throughout this book, but you wouldn't understand until you experience Him. The experience I had and am still having with God has sealed and cemented what I anticipate in my future. In other words, I am very confident in God about my future! Centuries ago, He made this promise by speaking through His prophet Jeremiah:

For I know the thoughts that I think toward you, saith the Lord, thought of peace, and not of evil, to give you an expected end.

JEREMIAH 29:11

It's not God's desire that anyone should be destroyed. However, the way that an individual chooses will decide their destiny. In this life, we observe and become acquainted with the laws of nature. One of nature's laws is the sowing and reaping strategy. Whatever seed is sown, the result will derive from the seed's nature.

Therefore, if a grain of corn is sown, the result will be stalk-bearing corn-not stalk-bearing beans. Now, as it is in the natural realm, it is in the spiritual. The Bible further states that whatever a man sows, he shall reap. [Galatians 6:7]. This means no one should be surprised or confused if they are conscious of how the law works naturally and spiritually. With all that has been said, embracing the fullness of life is impossible without injecting God into the picture. John the Beloved wrote to Gaius (a believer in Christ) that he wishes above all things that he may be prosperous and healthy even as his soul is prosperous. [3 John 1-2]. So, we see that life, in its most enigmatic form, is a tapestry interwoven with threads of spiritual quests and physical experiences. This intricate blend shapes our perception, guides our actions, and colors our interactions with the world and fellow human beings. The essence of existence, therefore, transcends the mere act of living. It encompasses a broader, more profound understanding and engagement with the spiritual and physical realms that define our journey through life.

When an individual encounters God, the experience is none like any other. When the Light of Christ shines within, you will see clearly and understand that your life has a purpose. This intimate and exceptional experience will change the whole ball game called life. Everything automatically becomes new when an individual takes on the name of Jesus in water baptism and is filled with the Holy Ghost and fire:

> *Therefore if any man be in Christ, he is a new creature: old things are passed away; behold, all things become new.*

> 2 CORINTHIANS 5:17

The unbeliever or the unsaved person cannot understand it- even if you try to explain. A new purpose for life has been conceived, and now you are about to sprout from the inside out! Many will see it and wonder. A separation then begins to happen. This is because you have been born into a new world, the Kingdom of Almighty God.

The peace and joy that come with this experience are inexplicable. Drug intoxication cannot be compared to this new birth experience. Rightfully, it's called 'drug intoxication because that's what it does after each intake of short highs, it gradually poisons and damages your internal structures. However, the Holy Ghost, on the other hand, brings unspeakable joy and glory that the half is unspoken of! If you are not basking in the glory of Almighty God today, then you are certainly missing out! Yes, you may have a ton of money or be broke as a church mouse, but if you don't have Jesus taking complete control of your life today, your life is still worthless. You may highly disapprove of this statement, but you will find out sooner or later that it is true.

We may implement temporary fixes for some critical issues in our lives, which may seem to last. Then we realize that these temporary fixes only make matters worse! This could also signify that our Heavenly Father pleads to fix it for us. For those who are without, would you allow Him into your life today? There is nothing to lose but a whole ton load to gain! We could have nothing in this world, but if we have Jesus, we have everything! This is not hype gospel (as some would think), though we could boast if we wanted to, only in the Lord. In the scriptures, David testifies thus:

> *My soul shall make her boast in the LORD: The humble shall hear thereof, and be glad. O magnify the LORD with me, and let us exalt his name together. I sought the LORD, and He heard me and delivered me from all my fears. They looked unto Him and were lightened: And their faces were not ashamed. This poor man cried, and the LORD heard Him and saved him from all his troubles.*

> PSALM 34:2-6

There you have it!- David testifies of the goodness of God. When I came to know Jesus, I realized I wasn't living. The experiences I had with Him are mind-blowing. I can't even begin to say. From miraculous healings to supernatural protection and provision. With Him comes Righteousness, Peace, and Joy in the Holy Ghost. How could one not accept the King of kings and The Lord of lords today? You don't have to worry about failing Him if you confess your sins, repent, and move away from them. He will keep and preserve you with His supernatural strength while teaching you His righteousness.

He loves you as much as He loves me or anyone else. If you want to talk to Him today, do it right now! No human being who has ever walked the face of the earth could live without God. However, there are different levels or dimensions of God. We barely got by after the fall and before Jesus Christ came to our rescue. When we accept the freedom he offers through salvation, we experience God's fullness in our lives even more significantly than before the fall! He has brought the child of God to a dimension that can only be described as

Joy unspeakable and full of glory!

1 PETER 1:8

One song said,

If you only knew the blessings that salvation brings, you'll never stay away!

Therefore, seeing that Almighty God has given us a taste of heaven, it behooves us to hold fast to it lest the evil one comes and snatches it away. The experience we have with God since the fullness of His light shone into our whole being is priceless! Those who know what I am talking about can shout Hallelujah now! Think about the first time you receive the Holy Ghost and speak in heavenly language! How was it? Did you manage to explain it to your peers? When the Holy Ghost came, that feeling of supernatural glory and enhancement prepared us for what is coming next. All who wait for Jesus Christ will be changed- from mortal to immortality. Are you ready? Are you excited?!

The Father's love for us is inexplicable. Time and again, he would blow the minds of His chosen people by popping up and surprising us with a blessing. Have you ever experienced God's grace? Or His unconditional love and healing power? When I first received Christ into my life, I had a little wart-like mold between the two middle fingers at the back of my right hand, which seems to be growing daily. This is because it was getting the proper blood flow that was causing it to grow. How I got this mold-like thing between my fingers was a mystery. I idly burned a plastic bag over a lighted candle as a teenager. The flame rapidly ran up the melting bag, and instead of letting go of the plastic, I flickered my hand, trying to let the melted portion fall. It did the opposite. The melted plastic curled and landed right between my fingers. Wheew!

The silly things that youngsters do! It grew into a wart-like scar that appeared to be increasing constantly. Not long afterward, I received Jesus Christ as my Lord and Savior. However, one day, I remembered how this scar came about as I looked between my fingers, and my faith was triggered. I Instantly Started to curse or rebuke this wart- like cyst in the name of Jesus Christ of Nazareth. I watched the wart fade every day until it disappeared completely! Wow! Isn't that amazing? God proved Himself to me in an insignificant thing, such as a little scar-like wart that I carelessly brought on myself. How much more a more significant situation such as cancer, HIV, Heart disease, and such alike? Each time I recall this situation, it gives me the confidence that if God doesn't solve a particular issue in my life, He has His reason not to. I conclude that nothing, absolutely nothing, is impossible to God.

I have so many testimonies that I may not even have the time to share them all in this book. Now, ladies and gentlemen, despite all these stories and testimonies, nothing can convince an individual more than having their own experience through faith in Jesus Christ. I could write tons and tons of books of God's miracles and signs, but if an individual lacks faith, they will never experience God in their life.

> But without faith, it is impossible to please Him: for he that cometh to God must believe that He is and that He is a rewarder of them that diligently seek Him.

HEBREWS 11:6

You have to first come to the acknowledgment that God is a Spirit. A spirit is invisible, which means that that being is in a different world or the invisible world. Despite this, God operates both in the physical and the invisible world.

Before the physical, God was there all by Himself in eternity! He was just there all the time, as the self-existent one. However, He formed man from the dust and brought him into existence, into a physical world. Thus, the only world that man is accustomed to is the physical or natural world. However, that doesn't necessarily mean that humans should be ignorant of their origin or the sovereignty of their creator, for that matter. Therefore, God sent forth His word so that man could acknowledge Him and what He requires of them.

So then faith cometh by hearing, and hearing by the word of God.

ROMANS 10:17

There is, therefore, no excuse for anyone who heard the word of God and didn't take heed. No one can outsmart God- all intelligence comes from Him. Therefore, He is the Master of all intelligent entities!

God will protect His children from all attacks intended to destroy them. One night, I was working as a security officer at a particular community in Broward, Florida, and had just taken my break. The parking lot at the clubhouse was intentionally scantily lighted, maybe for energy conservation. It was between 12:30 am- 1:00 am, and as I sat in my vehicle with the sunroof opened, I dozed off a little. Before I knew it, some 'dark entity' who had climbed into the car via the sunroof was trying to pin me down. As I felt the pressure of this demonic force bearing down on me, my subconsciousness was triggered, and I started pleading the blood of Jesus Christ in my mind. In a split second, this unscrupulous predator shot out of the vehicle like a bird fleeing from prey! The bullet moved from my subconsciousness to the chamber of my mouth as I woke up shooting the blood of Jesus against the adversary! If you say creepy, I agree. After all these years of spiritual warfare, I think I am getting used to handling creepy encounters. I thank God for the power, not only found in His name but also His blood.

And they overcame by the blood of the Lamb, and by the word of their testimony; and they loved not their lives unto death.

My experiences with my Heavenly Father since I first found him almost three decades ago are priceless. If I had the chance to choose again, I would choose this way. He has proved who He is to me, and that settles it. He has also brought to my awareness His opponent- entities that hide themselves in the shadows but cause havoc on fallen humanity. Do you see how critical it is to choose whose side you are on right now? If we are called by the name of the LORD, the Bible declares that we should depart from iniquity.

When we are obedient to His word, we should have no doubt who we are and who we belong to.

Abundant life awaits the believer who receives the whole gospel of Jesus Christ.

The joy and peace we constantly feel as we pine after Him cannot be compared to any pricey possession we could ever own here on earth!

There be many that say who will shew us any good? LORD, lift up the light of thy countenance upon us. Thou hast put gladness in my heart, more than in the time that their corn and their wine increased. I will both lay me down and sleep: For thou, LORD, only makest me dwell in safety.

PSALM 4:6-8

Many individuals have great riches and possessions, but the constant misery of their souls would not allow them to enjoy what they possess. When a child of God is being blessed, He causes that individual to be prosperous in all their ways.

As long as Israel obeys God's word, they are constantly blessed. God emphatically informed them through His servant Moses that they would be blessed in all aspects of their lives! This means starting from the core of their souls (perfect health and wellness) to their households, fields, and even their animals. [Deuteronomy 28:1-14]. Now, the heathen (unbelievers) that surrounded them did not experience this kind of blessing because they were not in covenant.

Nevertheless, a few individuals from other nations were not in the patriarchal covenant, so to speak, but were blessed. This is a sign to show humanity that the God who made the whole universe is not a respecter of persons, nor is He partial. God is always searching for someone whose intelligence is in tune with Him. Therefore, the first step is to acknowledge that there is a God. The next thing is to seek out what He desires of us.

> *The heavens declare the glory of God; And the firmament sheweth his handy work. Day unto day uttereth speech, and night unto night sheweth knowledge. There is no speech nor language, where their voice is not heard. Their line is gone out through all the Earth, and their words to the end of the world.*

> PSALM 19: 1-4

While the psalmist (David) meditated, he received a divine revelation. David looked into the heavens, and it was as if the elements were hollering at him; "Hey! David! There is a God! And He has created the whole universe! Do you know Him?!" Even the day and the night seemed to engage him also. By the time David could finish his meditation, his faith in the only true and living God would have been magnified because of this new revelation.

Living for God comes with many benefits, above and beyond. No one that has ever come to Christ has ever been disappointed. They may confess they couldn't keep up with the footmen or the horsemen, but no one can say that God isn't good. When the sun shines, it's both for the just and the unjust. No one can say it (the sunlight) didn't filter through the cracks of the doors or windows of their home! God's mercies and grace are open to everyone and anyone who chooses to follow Him. Someone might think, "Hmm, he sounds like a salesman." Well, yes, I am a salesman and a true one who is also a witness and has countless testimonies of the goodness of God!

The testimonies of God are true. He doesn't need anyone to lie for Him. If He says you are tall, and you know you are short, you will automatically begin to grow! Because God is in total control of everything, it's impossible for Him to lie. One songwriter says,

When I think of the goodness of Jesus and all He has done for me, my soul cries out, Hallelujah! Thank God for saving me!

Thus, everyone who has encountered God, has a testimony. You probably were dead broke and didn't know where the next meal was coming from, and instantly, God made way for provision. Or your rent was past due, and you just lost your job, but God caused you to receive a check in the mail. God allows real-life situations so His beloved ones can pay Him attention. God knows everything we need before we are even aware of it. As a child of the King, He has given every one of us a blank check to fill in the blanks.

God needs nothing, but we need Him. The air we breathe belongs to Him, the water we drink belongs to Him, and the food we eat also belongs to Him. Now, we could ask ourselves, "Is there anything we own?" This is the reason why it is foolish to be a boaster.

For we brought nothing into this world, and it is certain we can carry nothing out. And having food and raiment let us be therewith content.

1 TIMOTHY 6:7-8

The moral of the matter is that we are grateful for our existence, of God's provisions, and to fear Him and keep His commandments, for it is the whole duty of man. It hasn't changed since the beginning of time. Our whole life scenario will change when we discover why we are here. I got saved just around 22 years ago, and that's when I believed my life had truly begun. Things I'd never known before started infiltrating my mind, and my whole life situation began to change.

It is marvelous to experience the light of God shining into your whole being. I guarantee you, you will never be the same. The enemy tried very hard to prevent humanity from having this experience with their Creator. However, man has had that kind of experience before. Adam had great fellowship with God before the Fall. It is the same Devil that caused us all to fall and is now trying to block us from being restored. Now, my friend, do you see we are engaged in a spiritual battle for our souls? The enemy won't let up, and that's a fact. He knows the time is short, and many folks are waking up. Sadly, many are giving in to his trickery and seductive ways. Although God has promised us a 'more abundant life,' it doesn't come quickly. An opponent is preventing us from going in; thus, a war must be fought.

Spiritual warfare is not a walk in the park. "Why?" We are fighting against an enemy that is not visible to the eyes. This is like blindfolding martial arts. However, in this case, every blow we throw at the enemy will connect if we have the right weaponry or technique to fight.

Moreover, following the Master's instruction is paramount. He had gone through this kind of warfare before and had overcome them. Thus, we, too, can overcome through His blood. The blessings that salvation brings to humanity are like nothing the world has ever seen or experienced. The prophets and patriarchs of old had encountered Almighty God on many different levels and occasions. However, those occasions were sometimes temporary. Now, these patriarchs and prophets would have loved to experience what we have and are experiencing with Almighty God! Yes, my friend, it's God coming into our temple to reside!

When Jesus Christ came to us as the Messiah, He brought all the goodies from Heaven. As He hanged with His disciples, they had nothing to worry about. He could provide Everything they could ever want- from food to clothing, sheltering, protection, and healing for the body, etc. Wherever Jesus was, it was Heaven for these disciples. However, He knew He would not be with them in a temporary bodily form for long. Thus, He promised them the Comforter, which is the Holy Spirit of the living God:

Nevertheless, I tell you the truth; It is expedient for you that I go away: for if I go not away, the comforter will not come unto you; but if I depart, I will send him unto you. And when he is come, he will reprove the world of sin, and of righteousness, and of judgement: of sin because they believe not on me; of righteousness, because I go to my Father, and ye see me no more; of judgement, because the prince of this world is judged. I have yet many things to say unto you, but ye cannot bear them now. Howbeit when he, the Spirit of truth, is come, he will guide you into all truth: for he shall not speak of himself; but whatsoever he shall hear, that shall he speak: and he will shew you things to come. He shall glorify me: for he shall receive of mine and shall shew it unto you. All things that the Father hath are mine: therefore said I, that he shall take of mine, and shall shew it unto you. A little while, and ye shall not see me: and again, a little while, and ye shall see me, because I go to my Father.

JOHN 16:7-16

On the day of Pentecost (One of the major Jewish feasts, also called the Feast of Weeks), the same Comforter that Jesus had spoken of fell on them in an upper room in Jerusalem. The disciples had a supernatural encounter they had never experienced before. These disciples were gathered together as Jesus had instructed them when suddenly they heard the sound of a 'boisterous rushing wind.' They saw tongues of fire sat on every believer, and each could speak in languages they had never spoken before! Thus, they could communicate with their Jewish brethren (pilgrims of many different languages) scattered all over the Mediterranean. Talk about an incredible experience!

The onlookers that were gathered with them were appalled, and lacking proper explanation, they came to some frivolous conclusion:

And they were dwelling at Jerusalem Jews, devout men, out of every nation under heaven. Now when this was noised abroad, the multitude came together, and were confounded, because that every man heard them speak in his own language. And they were all amazed and marvelled. Saying one to another, Behold, are not all these which speak Galilaens? And how hear we every man in our tongue, where in we were born? Parthians, and Medes and Elamites, and the dwellers in Mesopotamia, and in Judea, and Cappadocia, in Pontus, and Aisa, Phrygia, and Pamphylia, in Egypt. And in the parts of Libya about Cyrene, and strangers of Rome, Jews and proselytes, Cretes and Arabians, we do hear them speak in our tongues the wonderful works of God. And they were all amazed, and were in doubt, saying one to another, what meanest this? Others mocking said, these men are full of new wine.

ACTS 2:5-13

CHAPTER 17

THE RECYCLING WILL SOON BE OVER

Have you ever thought about time and how we are governed by it? This thing is called time. Have you ever wondered if it will ever end? In the vast expanse of the celestial bodies, time is an immutable force governing the universe and guiding the destiny of all within its grasp. From the elements of the heavens that dance in eternal orbits to the fleeting moments of human existence, time weaves its intricate tapestry, leaving its mark on everything it touches. Yet, within the relentless march of time lies a paradoxical truth: while time gives rise to cycles of birth and decay, it also heralds an inevitable end.

How did time come about? You may ponder. The truth is that time started with the creation of all things. Yes, my friend, time was nowhere around until God created the heavens and the earth. Before time, there was eternity, and after time, eternity awaits on the other side! This tells us that time has a temporary lifespan. When time has accomplished its duty, then it will be tossed aside. This means that as eternity had passed the baton unto time, time would, in turn, pass the baton back to eternity. Wow! That's Awesome, isn't it? You might as well slap your neighbor and tell 'em' "neighbor, T-i-m-e, is running out of time!" Hallelujah! I feel like I am in a preaching mode right now! Let me stop before I get carried away! With that being said, are you ready for eternity? Believe it or not, it is undoubtedly upon us. It is full-time to be up and ready.

So, time continued to execute as a noisy up setter (causing things or events to happen suddenly and simultaneously) or a silent observer. Please make no mistake: in whatever mode time seems to be in, humanity is bound by its relentless march. From the cradle to the grave, individuals navigate the current of temporal existence, each moment a brushstroke on the canvas of eternity. Have you ever sat and observed a timepiece? No matter what shape it's being displayed in, the fact remains that time, in general, is still a cycle. Often, folks use this cliche about 'what goes around comes around' but have no idea it applies to almost everything governed by time! However, all these things are rapidly coming to an end. Now, because we have become accustomed to the rituals of life's cycle, we inadvertently think that everything is bound to be the same as we tread forward to the future. Many, unfortunately, become unaware and careless about what lies ahead regarding their fate. The Holy Scripture explicitly declares a day for man's trial.

It went further to say that everyone will be judged according to his works and the deeds done in their body. Now, when we look around us, we can see signs screaming at us that the end of time is near. For instance, from wars and rumors of wars to natural disasters and celestial phenomena, everything points toward that time when the very fabric of reality will be torn. Yes, it will be a time of reckoning when the deeds of humanity will be laid bare before the judgment seat of Almighty God. So, you see, my friend, that of all its majesty and splendor, time has an expiration date. As a flame devours the candle, so is time-consuming everything in its path. Soon, recycling will come to an end. In the twilight hours of

THE RECYCLING WILL SOON BE OVER

the whole universe, when the stars fade into the skies, the echoes of creation have long since died away, and time will reach its inevitable conclusion.

Almighty God described Himself as the First and the Last, the Beginning and the Ending. What does that mean, an individual may ask? He points out that 'all things' began with Him and will inevitably end with Him. In other words, He is the Author and the Finisher of the documentary, and the lifetime and real-time movie of the most excellent book ever written- the 'Book of Earth.' No doubt about it. He is the Master director. Thus, He causes everything to happen in time. Living things (including humans) conceive and give birth in time. All living things die after some time (called lifespan) and return to the earth. From the smallest atoms to the most fantastic galaxy, all things are subject to the ever-immutable progression of time.

Now, as the sands of time slip through the hourglass of eternity, let us take heed of the signs of the end and prepare ourselves for the inevitable day of reckoning that awaits us all. For in the final moments of existence, when the recycling ends and time itself draws to a close, may we find solace in the knowledge that we have lived our lives with purpose and meaning as we prepare to meet the Master of time and our Creator, Almighty God. Many individuals today are so caught up with the gratification of the moment that they forget that amid life, eternity could snap!

In the book of Amos 4:12, the prophet warned the people of Israel to prepare to meet their God. Since God is the God of all nations, people, and creeds, then everyone should be ready to meet Him:

> *And I saw a great white throne, and Him that sat on it, from whose face the earth and the heaven fled away; and there was found no place for them. And I saw the dead, small and significant, stand before God, and the books were opened: and another book was opened, which is the book of life: and the dead were judged out of those things which were written in the books, according to their works. And the sea gave up the dead which were in it, and death and hell delivered up the dead which were in them: and they were judged every man according to their works. And death and hell were cast into the lake of fire. This is the second death. And whosoever was not found written in the book of life was cast into the lake of fire.*

REVELATION 11: 15

Now, these Scriptures indeed refer to what lies ahead for everyone who has ever existed since the world began. According to the Bible, no one is exempt:

For we must all appear before the judgment seat of Christ; that everyone may receive the things done in his body, according to that he hath done, whether it be good or bad.

2 CORINTHIANS 5

So, let me ask you, reader, are you excited to see our soon-coming king, or are you withdrawn with doubts and regrets? If it's the latter, you still have time to fix this. If you are breathing and conscious, you can still confess to Him all your sins, repent, and embrace God's grace, love, and fantastic freedom.

I must say, as children of the most High God, many unbelievers would want to think that we sound like a typical salesperson. The problem is that what we are advertising is not for sale! Moreover, the only one who would get the glory out of this is who called, charged, and sent us- Almighty God, our master and savior. The Psalmist in Psalm 34:8 declares:

O taste and see that the Lord is good: Blessed is the man that trusteth in Him.

Our duty (those of us baptized in Jesus' name and filled with the Holy Ghost) is to spread the gospel's good news. We all know what we experience when we come to Christ:

That the trial of your faith, being much more precious than of gold that perisheth, though it be tried with fire, might be found unto praise and honor and glory at the appearing of Jesus Christ: who having not seen, ye love; in whom, though ye see Him not, yet believing, ye rejoice with joy unspeakable and full of glory:
receiving the end of your faith, even the salvation of your souls.

The scripture undeniably declares it, and I am a faithful witness.

When I came to Jesus Christ, I was filled with fear, doubt, and hopelessness. If you can recall my story (I've written earlier in this book), he drew me to him, using other individuals. God can feel your pains, worries, and fears wherever you are. If you sincerely cry out to Him for help, He will quickly come to your rescue. So, back to what I said, my life was empty and void. However, I knew it, but I couldn't figure out the right solution- even though there's always that gut feeling that the church may have that solution you are looking for. Many of us look to the house of God as the last resort to solve life's problems. But why is that so anyway? Is it because we think it is a place of restriction, or is it too old-fashioned? Whatever the answer, Jesus is the only solution for all our problems; He is the same yesterday, today, and over. The word of God declares that there is nothing new under the sun. This tells us that everything is a cycle. First thing in the morning, we headed to the bathroom, refreshed ourselves, had breakfast (those of us who do), and then headed to work or the gym, etc. The next day, we start the process all over again. Our ritualistic life, habits, and activities never seem to stop, but one day, it will soon be over.

The false concept that this present world will continue forever is delusional. The complacency of being satisfied with this world of wickedness is like a time bomb ready to explode! Children of God must be aware of the time we are living in. The Word of God states that we are children of light and the day; we are not of the night nor darkness. [1 Thessalonians 5:5]. God's children must be watchful and vigilant. We should never act or make decisions based on worldview. We may be in a physical body, but we are spiritual beings. The outer- man will soon be dissolved, and the inner- man will be revealed. When humanity fails to believe and honor God's word, a set time of judgement is imminent. On that note, let us examine ourselves and see whether we are in the faith or not.

We must constantly evaluate ourselves to see if we are in the right standing with God. As lively stones, we must always be ready to kindle a spiritual fire in someone's life. The time is too short for Christians to attend or even throw pity parties. There is no time for such things. A die-hard child of God must be ready to slap the devil off a victim. Many folks (even our family members sometimes) who are not familiar with spiritual warfare may be undergoing some issues and looking for a solution. They would sometimes become overwhelmed, and instead of looking towards God for the solution, they threw a pitiful tantrum. This is where a radical child of God must step in and knock the wind out of that old dragon.

Too many people are walking around throwing pity parties as if God is dead. Someone needs to know that there is a God who is alive and kicking, and the devil is a dirty old liar! The recycling will soon be over, my friend, and if we are not ready to meet our Creator, what awaits us is a hopeless eternity. We've got to go hard or don't go at all. Hell's gate needs to burst open, and the captives need to be set free. Hell's prisoners are walking around like zombies in shackles and chains of darkness. Like David charging at Goliath, we should have that warrior-like spirit pouncing impatiently to engage the adversary. The day is breaking, and some poor, fainting soul is about to be lost. The time will come when there is no more getting up and heading to work or the field to plow the ground. It is bearing down on us, and we can feel the shift in the atmosphere. At the midnight cry, nothing will be the same anymore. The next big thing in the History of humanity is not any wars or rumors of wars, or a great flood (like in the days of Noah), nor an earthquake or the usual destructions and disasters that happened in the past- but it's the snatching away (some called it 'the rapture') of the people of God!

> *But I would not have you to be ignorant, brethren, concerning them which are asleep, that ye sorrow not, even as others which have no hope. For if we believe that Jesus died and rose again, even so them also which sleep in Jesus will God bring with Him. For this we say unto you by the word of the Lord, that we which are alive and remain unto the coming of the Lord shall not prevent them which are asleep. For the Lord Himself shall descend from heaven with a shout, with the voice of the archangel, and with the trump of God: and the dead in Christ shall rise first: then we which are alive and remain shall be caught up together with them in the clouds, to meet the Lord in the air: and so shall we ever be with the Lord. Wherefore comfort one another with these words.*

1 THESSALONIANS 4: 13-18

Nothing can stop God's plan and intentions for this world and His people. No one, dead or alive, can prevent Him from accomplishing His will. Whether you are a believer or an infidel, God's conceived plan must be executed. The church will be raptured before any major events occur or conspire by the Prince of Darkness. The church or the bride of Christ is the one that's preventing the prince of darkness from appearing. Can you imagine what will happen when the church is no longer around? The devil's witches, wizards, magicians, and sorcerers are already manifesting more than ever. They are all over social media and are unafraid to showcase their power! I must say, if you come across this book and happen to be one of these individuals, get out of it now! Repent of all your sins immediately and ask God for forgiveness. All these powers are from the pit of hell and are influenced by demonic entities. There are no powers or demons in Hell greater than Almighty God. [Romans 13:1-2].

Therefore, when the church is taken up, then all hell will be let loose on earth! The church will not be around for these events. Jesus is not coming for a beat-up bride- but for one who is vibrant and without spots or wrinkles! The trials of the church will soon be over. Will you be there on the other side? The anti-Christ cannot push his ugly head up until the church is out of sight. Those who are left behind will be prone to great deception. This is because there will be no Holy Spirit to lead anyone into any truth or righteousness. Yes, my friend, it's going to be dreadful for those who are left behind. Deceptions will be everywhere:

Remember ye not, that, when I was yet with you, I told you these things? And now ye know what witholdeth that he might be revealed in his time. For the mystery of iniquity doth already work: only he who letteth will let, until he be taken out of the way.

And then shall the Wicked be revealed, whom the Lord shall consume with the spirit of His mouth, and shall destroy with the brightness of His coming: even him, whose coming is after the working of Satan with all power and signs and lying wonders, and with all deceivableness of unrighteousness in them that perish; because they received not the love of the truth, that they might be saved. And for this cause, God shall send them strong delusion, that they should believe a lie: That they all might be damned who believed not the truth, but had pleasure in unrighteousness.

2 THESSALONIANS 2:5-12

Do you see how important it is to make it in the rapture? God's word has already outlined the events about to hit Earth. Do you believe in the word of God, written through the inspiration of the Holy Ghost? Or will you allow yourself to be deceived by some delusional, disorganized thoughts, concepts, religions, or philosophies?

Receiving Jesus Christ in one's life is not merely a kind of religion, as some put it, but an experience. True Christianity is a lifetime of spiritual experiences. There is no substitute for the Apostle's doctrine, the foundation we build on, with Jesus Christ as the chief cornerstone. That's it! There is no other way of escaping the pending judgment about to hit the Earth. Many anticipate peace and safety, but little do they know that sudden destruction awaits the unprepared. There is a time for everything under the heavens, and the time for God to take back what rightfully belongs to Him (the worlds, including the universe and everything in them) has come. As recycling is about to end, our spiritual sight should be more alert than ever. The whole earth is now weary of the pressure imposed upon it by the wicked force of darkness:

> *For we know the whole creation groaneth and travaileth in pain together until now. And not only they, but ourselves also, which have the first fruit of the Spirit, even we ourselves groan within ourselves, waiting for the adoption, to wit, the redemption of our body.*

ROMANS 8: 22-23

The recycling will soon be over, and a new era will be ushered in. What a day that will be! However, there will be some significant days before the replenishment. A few prophets foresaw the Day of the Lord and were appalled by what it entails. Seeing that the Day of the Lord is rapidly approaching, it behooves us to 'make hay while the sun shines.' Preparing and being ready for what is about to happen is the best solution.

The strange things happening around us are sending us a message that something great and supernatural is about to happen. The signs of the time are appearing everywhere. No one will escape. Knowing that the Scriptures have already forewarned us, those in Christ should not be confused about what will occur. Moreover, as the Bible suggests, 'the church' will not be in the melee when these events start happening. God permanently secures His people before destruction comes; Noah and his family of seven (his wife, his three sons, and their wives), along with a slew of paired animals, entered the Ark before the great flood; Joshua and his colleagues rescued rehab and her family before Jericho was utterly destroyed; and finally Lot, his wife and two daughters were rescued by two angels before Sodom and Gomorrah were pelted from above with brimstone and fire.

Now Jesus warned His disciples what would happen in the last days:

> But of that day and hour knoweth no man, no, not the angels of heaven, but my Father only. But as the day of Noe were, so shall also the coming of the Son of man be. For as in the days that were before the flood they were eating and drinking, marrying and giving in marriage, until the day that Noe entered the ark, and knew not until the flood came, and took them all away; so shall also the coming of the Son of man be. Then shall two be in the field; the one shall be taken, and the other left. Two women shall be grinding at the mill; the one shall be taken, and the other left.

MATTHEW 24:36-41

Know this one thing, my friend: no one knows when the rapture will happen. Still, we know of a fact (by studying, rightly dividing, and understanding): the word of God will take place before the Tribulation, which is seven gruesome years on Earth under the cruelty of the antichrist. The church will be gone to be with the bridegroom, and a new era will begin, called the millennium. The door will be opened once more for the people of God to acknowledge and accept their Messiah. Of course, they will be deceived by the antichrist, who will be pretending to be their messiah for three and half years before his deception is revealed.

CHAPTER 18
WHO GOD IS?

Throughout the annals of history, many individuals rigorously attempted to seek, find out, and know God. Unfortunately, their effort most of the time proved futile, and eventually, many raised false deities, and some even became atheists out of sheer ignorance. Now, why is that so? Some of us would have a boss or a so-called superior if we were an employee, right? For instance, if you are on a job for the first time and have never met the boss before, you probably would want to, but don't even know the location of their office. Now, say, for example, your boss has an office only specific individuals can access. Do you think that that office door will always open for anyone to walk right in to see the boss? Absolutely not. Often, as a regular employee, there are rules and protocols that you must follow to meet the boss. Not following these rules and protocols would be considered a violation.

Therefore, the same situation applies to the only Supreme Being that created the universe. Firstly, we must understand that a Superior or Supreme Being (One that is above all) is what we call God. Now, who is that Supreme Being- God? According to the Holy Bible in the Book of John [John 4:24], Jesus (God Incarnate or God in the flesh) explicitly explains to the woman at the well that God is a Spirit. Many times, in the Holy Scriptures of the Old Testament and the New alike, there are instances where the term 'The Spirit of God' is mentioned. When the Holy Scriptures mention the 'Spirit of God,' it merely refers to 'that invisible state of God that we cannot see with the physical eyes.' However, being the unique and Supreme Being that

He is, God has features and attributes that far supersede that of humans. Thus, understanding God's attributes is vital to grasping His essence.

The Bible attributes several characteristics to God:

- **Omnipotence**: God is all-powerful, capable of doing anything in harmony with His nature.
- **Omniscience**: God is all-knowing, fully aware of the past, present, and future, including the most profound thoughts and intentions of every heart.
- **Omnipresence**: God is in all places at all times, not confined by space or time, yet in a way that transcends mere physical presence.
- **Omnibenevolence**: God is all-good, the source of all love, mercy, and grace, seeking the ultimate good of His creation.

As I mentioned before, access to God is not a freeway. In the Holy Scriptures of the Old Testament, individuals who desire to know God must give up some, if not all, things to gain that intimate fellowship. However, there is no going back once you have gone beyond that veil or partition. This does not mean that you will know all there is to know about Him, or you suddenly become a superhuman. He is too magnificent for us to know everything about Him! Most prophets or patriarchs who encountered God in His glory fell flat before Him without strength. As the saying goes, this little lump of clay cannot stand all the fullness of Almighty God! So, to tone things down, God provided Himself with a body.

Before going there, we must understand that He is just one Supernatural being- not two or three! Whew! Pause, take a deep breath, and let that sink in.

Ok, are you still breathing? Good. To make Himself known to humanity, Almighty God must communicate. Of course, as humans, we know that there are different ways of communicating. However, God chose to speak through His Word (the Holy scripture), the patriarchs, the prophets of old, and through His Holy Spirit, to name a few. In the Book of 2 Peter 1: 20-21, Peter declares that the scripture didn't derive from man's private, personal agenda or craftiness but from holy men who have committed or sacrificed their lives unto God. On this note, let us turn our attention to the book of Deuteronomy 6:4, which states thus:

> *Hear, O Israel: The Lord our God is one Lord: and thou shalt love the Lord thy God with all thine heart, and with all thy soul, and with all thy might.*

This statement in Hebrew is known as the 'Shema Prayer' and confirms what God told Moses during his first encounter with God from the burning bush: [Exodus 3:14].

> *And God said unto Moses, I AM THAT I AM: and he said, thus shalt thou say unto the children of Israel, I AM hath sent me unto you.*

This is emphatically applied because Almighty God wants to clarify that He alone is God and there is none else besides Him [Isaiah 45:5]. So now we see that there shouldn't be any confusion about who the only true God is. However, to execute His plan in the heavenly and the earthly realms, He must manifest or reveal Himself differently. The same God can reveal Himself in various forms, shapes, and ways! Are you still not yet convinced? Consider the Old Testament scriptures: [Genesis 18:1-2, Exodus 3:2, 1 King 19:12].

The Old Testament presents God as the Creator of the universe who forms a special covenant with Abraham, promising to make his descendants a great nation. Through this covenant, and later through Moses and the law, God reveals His nature as just, faithful, and merciful. Despite humanity's repeated failures, God remains committed to His covenant, displaying patience and providing for His people's redemption.

So now we see that God is the One and Only Supreme Being of the universe (executing His divine plan all by Himself); let us look into His manifestation in the New Testament to accomplish the task He first initiated. The New Testament shifts the focus to fulfilling God's promise through Jesus Christ (God robing Himself in the flesh and dwelling with us). Here, we see God's entire operations, working in the offices of the Father (which is the Spirit), the Son (which is the flesh or bodily form), and the Holy Ghost (which is the rebirth or regenerative power) to transform us into sons of God. The One and Only, true God is in complete execution simultaneously: [Isaiah 63:5]. What an awesome God He is!

The Gospels—Matthew, Mark, Luke, and John—offer diverse perspectives on Jesus's life and ministry, his teachings on the kingdom of God, his miracles, and his sacrificial death and resurrection. Through Jesus, God's kingdom is inaugurated on earth, inviting all into a life-transforming relationship with God. In the book of 1 Timothy 3:16, the Bible declares:

> *And without controversy great is the mystery of godliness: God was manifest in the flesh, justified in the Spirit, seen of angels, preached unto the world, received up into glory.*

After Jesus's ascension, the Holy Ghost is sent to empower and guide the former and latter churches. The Acts of the Apostles and the epistles provide insight into how the Holy Ghost worked within communities to spread the gospel, forge unity, and nurture believers' spiritual growth. The role of the Holy Spirit is pivotal in enabling the church to understand and live out the teachings of Jesus and reveal God's incredible power and presence in the world.

Now that we clearly understand who God is, those of you who are not yet saved, are you willing to take the initiative to receive Him as your Lord and Savior? Have you been baptized in the name of Jesus Christ of Nazareth, which is above every name? Or even receive the infilling of the Holy Ghost? Do you have the power to overcome and break the chains of the enemy of your soul- that keep humanity in bondage since the introduction of sin? If you answer no or are uncertain of this freedom in Christ Jesus, start running to him immediately! His arms are wide open and ready to receive you. He has long waited for you to repent and turn your heart towards him. Please, do it now without delay.

The Holy Ghost is the only way an individual can see God today. The Holy Ghost, the comforter that Jesus promised He would send after He ascended, fell on the disciples on the day of Pentecost. The Spirit of God came like a mighty rushing wind and sat on every one of them, and they were all filled with the Holy Ghost and fire. Again, we can see that God does not leave His people hopeless. The church is not a feeble entity but the beloved bride of Christ. The Spirit of God is also present where the' church' is. He promised His disciple: "Lo I am with you always, even unto the end of the world. This tells me that Jesus Christ is God manifested in the flesh! That is, the only God who possesses the features of omnipotence, omniscient, and omnipresence can make that statement. No one else can or ever will! Jesus (Immanuel, which means God is with us) was here on earth and at the same time monitoring the affairs of the universe! How awesome and unfathomable is that! Who can figure God out? - No one!

As we claim to get closer and closer to God as His beloved children, we begin to see that the magnitude of His glory and greatness is almost unbearable. There is always something new about God. His ways are past finding out. So-called great men tried to fathom His greatness but to no avail! Some even came to a disappointing conclusion and decided there was no God. How absurd is this situation?! God is not obliged to show Himself to anyone- and even if He chooses to do so, who can stand it? Which one of His prophets or holy men could stand before Him once he showed up in His glory? The children of Israel scampered away when they saw the glory of God touch down on the Mount. It was too unbearable for them. [Exodus 20: 18].

Even though many are aware of this fact (the existence and greatness of Almighty God), they continue to live in their rebellious and crooked ways. However, a day of reckoning is approaching rapidly, and everyone will be accountable for their life here on Earth. The mere fact that when one dies, they often die alone tells us that everyone is responsible for the time they spend here on Earth. We all have our time, and without a doubt, God has everything organized and filed in the filing cabinet of heaven. No one will escape! In this troubling world, men tend to change their identity from time to time. Sometimes, because of some negative situations that happened in their life. At other times, they just wanted to be someone else. Whatever the cause, the way that person was born originally is written down in the history book of heaven!

According to the book of Matthew 10 29, when a sparrow dies, its death doesn't go unnoticed. Yes, my friend, God acknowledges every minute detail we can think of. Nothing escapes His eyes. If we choose not to serve God by not trusting and obeying His will, then there is no other help or hope for us. That's it; God answers to no one else but Himself. He rules all, controls all, and is sovereign overall. Nothing or no one can stop God from doing whatever He pleases. His mercies and grace are what keep us daily. His kindness and love for humanity are seen when the sun sets in the evening and rises afresh in the morning.

God's intention for all humanity is seen in the great work that He wrought for us on Calvary. Up to that point in time, humanity's (God's people, the children of Israel) substitute for sin and trespasses was the slaying of goats, rams, sheep, doves, bullocks, etc. These were sacrificed as sin offerings according to the measure of their trespasses. However, there was a sin offering (a sacrifice made every year) for all the sins an individual does throughout the year. Everyone must bring a lamb for a sin offering. When Jesus came on the scene, He came as God incarnate or the ultimate sacrificial lamb for all humanity. In John 3:16, the bible declares:

For God so loved the world, that he gave his only begotten Son, that whosoever believeth in Him should not perish, but have everlasting life.

There goes the character of God! Because of never- failing and unconditional love, God came off His throne robe Himself in the flesh and came to rescue the soul of fallen humanity. God's unchanging love sustains the Earth, preserves humanity, and keeps back the onslaught of the destroyer. You cannot escape from the love of God.

Someone would say, but why would God have to do all this? - to restore us to our previous state- so we can be reconciled to Him. Just imagine, if Adam wasn't turned out of the garden, they would have stretched forth their hands and reached for the Tree of Life. What happened next would have been catastrophic for all of Adam's generations, including us. In their fallen and sinful state, they would have been defaulted and, therefore, become like devils and demons! Thus, we would have been chopped off from God forever. This is because of His Pure and Holy character. To live and dwell in God's presence forever, we must adapt to the same wavelength, and our minds must be in sync with His:

> *Let this mind be in you, which was also in Christ Jesus: who, being in the form of God, thought it not robbery to be equal with God.*

PHILIPPIANS 2:6

To be in disharmony with God is a threat to His kingdom- sounds familiar. God would have to prove to the devil and his thugs that there is only but One God and Creator of all things both in heaven, on Earth, beneath the Earth, and the whole universe! It is good to seek God with a heart of humility. A spirit of pride will not cut. Lucifer was basking in his glory, thinking he was the hottest thing. Indeed, God is a God that hides Himself from time to time. He is not a puppet or a toy that one could put in a box and pull out when convenient. Thus, Lucifer didn't know the magnitude of the greatness of Almighty God.

If Satan knew, he would have never thought of pitching his throne above the stars and to be like the most High God. Eventually, his ignorance cost him everything- a war took place in heaven, and he was cast out:

> *And there was war in heaven: Michael and his angels fought against the dragon, and the dragon fought and his angels and prevailed not; neither was their place found anymore in heaven. And the great dragon was cast out, that old serpent, called the Devil, and Satan, which deceiveth the whole world: he was cast out into the earth, and his angels were cast out with him.*

REVELATION 12: 7-9

The prophet Isaiah also confirmed this in the Old Testament of the Holy Scriptures:

> *How art thou fallen from heaven, O Lucifer, son of the morning! How art thou cut down to the ground, which didst weaken the nations! For thou hast said in thine heart, I will ascend into heaven; I will exalt my throne above the stars of God: I will sit also upon the mount of the congregation, in the sides of the north: I will ascend above the heights of the clouds; I will be like the most High. Yet thou shalt be brought down to hell, to the sides of the pit.*

ISAIAH 14: 12-15

God will neither share nor give His glory to another. There is only one God with absolute power, and He is about to prove this to the world! Many times, in history, even up to this point, great men rose, claiming to be mighty and strong. Some even blaspheme the name of God but were brought down miserably, eventually.

Whatever the influence was on these men, it makes no difference. Jesus (Yahweh) is God and always will be. One of the strategies the opponent of our God uses is bribery. The Devil's agenda is to find a victim who is ready and available to scheme his dirty plans. However, it doesn't matter how reckless and outrageous these abject seem; they must eventually submit to a higher power.

Wherefore God also hath highly exalted him and given him a name which is above every name: that at the name of Jesus, every knee should bow, of things in heaven, and things in earth, and things under the earth; and that every tongue should confess that Jesus Christ is Lord, to the glory of God the Father.

PHILIPPIANS 2: 9-11

Now, because our God doesn't readily reveal Himself to anyone (because of His Holiness), Many individuals have different thoughts and concepts about God. Some even suggested that nature is God. However, if we go back to the Bible and how it all started, we will realize that all other concepts, ideas, and philosophical clout do not cut. The Bible explicitly gives an account of God being there before everything ever existed, of Him creating the Heaven and the Earth, and of His unique features and phenomenal character. God owes no one any explanation. If it feels fit or necessary for us to know certain things about this life, natural or spiritual, He will reveal it to us. Otherwise, He has no obligations.

Nevertheless, God controls everything, even though He is not visibly being seen. He still rules in the kingdom of men. God fills the whole universe; there is nowhere for Him to go. There is nowhere on Earth or in Heaven where He is not!

Thus saith the Lord, the heaven is my throne, and the earth is my footstool: Where is the house that ye build unto me? And where is the place of my rest? For all those things hath mind hand made, and all those things have been saith the Lord:

ISAIAH 66: 1-2

God is not a god that can be tucked in a box or closet for future use! He is the only sovereign and intelligent being who knows even the very thoughts of the mind.

When an individual is filled with the Holy Ghost, He can discern, detect, and do things he has never done before. Notwithstanding, the Spirit of God works and operates in man to do the supernatural. He told the prophet to tell the people of Israel that whatever He was about to do was not by might or power but by His Spirit. [Zechariah 4:6]. God is present everywhere, knows everything, is all-powerful, and cannot be restricted by anything or anyone. That thought alone should have us taking inventory of our lifestyle, habits, and attitude toward God and man. The Bible says that we will be judged accordingly. God is seen as our Shepherd (the good shepherd), and we are His sheep. Now, sheep cannot just go roaming alone- a shepherd must guide them. Sheep don't have any sense of direction. When sheep go astray, it's a probability that they might encounter some danger in the wild. A wild beast or predator may lurk nearby, or a precipice may be a few feet away.

Because of their nature, sheep must always be attended to, whatever the circumstance. Thus, the shepherd must implement some restrictive measures to safeguard the sheep. To prevent self-destruction, sheep must have boundaries! According to the Bible,

> *All we like sheep have gone astray; we have turned everyone to his own way, and the LORD hath laid on Him the iniquity of us all.*

ISAIAH 53:6

Despite man being given free will, we must be guided and monitored. However, our thought process is that we can do everything independently and even care for our needs without external intervention. Unfortunately, we weren't designed that way. There are certain things that are just beyond man's comprehension.

This is where the Good Shepherd intervened. God, who made and formed man from the dust, knew that we could not do without Him. We were designed to be dependent on our Superior, which is God. His very breath was infused into us when we were lifeless! This tells me we are unique beings, and His DNA runs through our veins.

> *God that made the world and all things therein seeing that He is LORD of heaven and of earth, dwelleth not in temples made with hands, neither is worshipped with men's hands, as though He needed anything, seeing that He giveth to all life and breath, and all things; and hath made of one blood all nations of men for to dwell on all the face of the earth, and hath determined the times before appointed, and the bounds of their habitation; that they should seek the LORD if haply they might feel after Him, and find Him, though He be not far from every one of us: for in Him we live, and move and have our being; as certain of your own poets have said, For we are also His offspring.*

ACTS 17:24-28

The express image of God is Jesus Christ. When we experience Jesus in our lives, we have encountered God himself. Many of us who haven't received the revelation may see Jesus separate from God. However, that would be contrary to scriptures found in the Old and New Testaments concerning the deity of God. Jesus told the woman at the well that God is a spirit, and they that worship must worship in spirit and truth. [John 4:24]. "Now, if God is a Spirit, how is Jesus tied in with God?" someone may ask. Well, a spirit does not have flesh and blood as humans do. Therefore, God must find some way to make Himself visible to man! Remember that God can present Himself or even appear in different forms! The Devil is a copycat and possesses this kind of ability despite being restricted. God chose the Image of Jesus Christ to reveal Himself to man, who reflects the same! The Image cannot exist without the Spirit, but the Spirit existed before the Image.

The Image of God does not necessarily conclude the magnitude of God's greatness, though His fullness is contained therein. Nonetheless, it is the Image that He chose to tabernacle or live in! The Spirit of God is not confined to the Body or Image (of Christ), but the Image or the Body is confined to the Spirit! Solomon had a hint of this during his prayer when he remembered the LORD's response concerning his father David, who desired to build a temple for God:

> And now, O God of Israel, let thy word, I pray thee, be verified, which thou spakest unto thy servant David, my father. But will God indeed dwell on the earth? Behold the heaven and heavens of heavens cannot contain thee; how much this house that I have builded?

> 1 KINGS 8: 26-27

I conclude that it is impossible to know the deep and glorious things of Almighty God by just scratching the surface. Moses could only attain more from God by obeying His command to come up into the cloud! Too often, folks want to know more about God but do not want to pay the price. Yes, there is a price to pay for living close to God. This requires complete self-denial- a lifestyle of sacrifice. It's the oath of a spiritual warrior! Why not be enlisted? God is always calling us to a higher dimension.

> Deep calleth unto deep at the noise of thy waterspouts: All thy waves and thy billows are gone over me.

> PSALMS 42:7

CHAPTER 19

THE CLOSING OF THE LAST DAYS

The concept of "The Last Days" has fascinated and intrigued scholars, theologians, and believers for centuries. Defined within the Christian tradition as the period leading up to the Second Coming of Christ, the Last Days are characterized by prophetic events, signs, and changes within human society and the natural world. The Holy Scriptures, especially in books such as Daniel, Matthew, and Revelation, offer a framework for understanding these times, describing signs preceding the end of the age. As the world undergoes rapid economic, technological, and societal shifts, many wonder whether these changes align with the prophetic markers outlined in Scripture. Let us explore the intersection of biblical prophecy and current global trends without further ado and decide whether we are witnessing the closing of the last days.

The Bible outlines several key prophecies regarding the end times, serving as markers for the Last Days. In the book of Daniel, visions of beasts and kings symbolize empires and events unfolding through history, culminating in the final kingdom before the establishment of God's eternal reign. Matthew 24, as spoken by Jesus, details signs such as wars, famines, earthquakes, and the gospel's spread to all nations, which are to precede His return. With its rich symbolism, Revelation speaks of the rise of the Antichrist, the mark of the beast, and great tribulations. Though some of these prophecies, spoken by the prophets and even by Jesus Himself, have already been fulfilled, many are yet to be manifested. Things seemed to intensify around us as we approached the end of the Last Days. However, examining the current global crisis through the lens of these prophecies, we can see several fulfilled events. The increase in biblical lawlessness, which includes illicit sex, violence, deceit, earthquakes in diverse places, famine, murder, war, and rumors of war (just to name a few), mirrors the "birth pains" described in Matthew 24.

However, the global spread of Christianity, despite increasing persecution in various parts of the world, aligns with the prophecy of the gospel reaching all nations. Additionally, the moral decay and societal upheaval witnessed in recent times reflect the foretold lawlessness and cooling of love among many. The global economy exhibits several trends that resonate with biblical warnings about the Last Days. Economic instability, evidenced by fluctuating markets, inflation, and the increasing gap between the wealthy and the poor, mirrors the tumultuous conditions forewarned for these times. The shift towards digital currencies and the potential for global economic systems point to a future where buying and selling could be controlled, as suggested in the prophecy regarding the mark of the beast in Revelation. While offering numerous economic benefits, technological advancement aligns with biblical prophecies concerning control and surveillance in the Last Days. The development of global surveillance networks, data tracking, and digital identification systems could be precursors to world control described in Revelation 13. The rapid advancement in artificial intelligence and biotechnology raises ethical questions and potential scenarios where humanity's freedom could be significantly constrained, reflecting concerns expressed in biblical prophecy. At this present time, we are living in a moral and spiritual landscape that is characterized by a notable decline, a condition that the Bible associates with the Last Days. This decline is evident in the widespread acceptance and normalization of behaviors once considered immoral, the diminishing influence of traditional religious values in public life, and the rise of a cultural ethos that prioritizes individualism over community and relativism over absolute truth. These trends also reflect the apostasy and love growing cold, as Jesus mentioned in Matthew 24.

In these challenging times, the role of the church and individual believers has become increasingly critical. The Bible calls for vigilance, perseverance in faith, and a commitment to spreading the gospel. We are encouraged to "look up" and remain watchful, interpreting the signs of the times through a biblical lens. The church is also tasked with providing hope, guidance, and support to those navigating the uncertainties of these days, fulfilling its mission as a beacon of light in a darkening world.

Preparation for the Last Days involves both spiritual and practical dimensions. Spiritually, we, as believers, are called to deepen our spiritual relationship with God through prayer, fasting, studying the Scriptures, and living out our faith authentically in everyday life. Preparing involves wise stewards of resources, fostering strong community ties, and developing resilience to face challenges. Such preparation is not driven by fear but by a desire to stand firm in faith, regardless of circumstances. Despite the challenges and uncertainties of the Last Days, the Bible offers profound hope and assurance for believers. The culmination of these events leads to the glorious return of Jesus Christ, the establishment of His kingdom, and the restoration of all things. Believers are encouraged to keep their focus on this eternal perspective, finding peace and strength in the promises of God. The message of Revelation ends with a note of hope:

> *He who testifies to these things says, 'Yes, I am coming soon.' Amen. Come, Lord Jesus.*

Now, with all that being said, my friend, are you ready for the coming of the Lord? Are you aware of the signs of the time? Indeed, That Day will Come- it is the great day of the Lord. It is a day of reckoning and judgment. Each day we wake up, there is always something new, some new events and discoveries. As we advance toward the end of days, everything around us intensifies. We can see that violence appears to increase, the cost of living is outrageous, and disasters unheard of are happening almost everywhere. More people are dying of sicknesses, starvation, and hunger. The signs of the time are screaming out to us that something big is about to happen- a divine intervention is about to occur. The more these signs steer us in the face, the more individuals become numb about what is happening around them. Many think that if these things don't affect them, their loved ones, and associates, then everything is alright.

We live in a world where people could care less about the order of the day. Nevertheless, it's up to us not to think as the majority do. The word of God stated that when they should say peace and safety, then sudden destruction comes upon them as travail upon a woman with a child. [1 Thessalonians 5:3]. Most individuals are ok with their way of living because everything seems to be going smoothly. Unfortunately, many never stop to think that life will not always be the same. Yes, my friend, there is a new day dawning; being prepared is the only way to escape.

Glancing at our time clock, we see that prophecies are fulfilled daily. God's plan for His world and His people will never fail. Nothing has ever or will ever stop Almighty God from executing His will in heaven and here on Earth. [Matthew 6:10, Luke 11:12]. Many of us are planning for the future (as this book is being read), but are we certain of the next moment, much less tomorrow? True warriors of the cross live as if today is the last day. We all should have a certain level of consciousness about God's imminent return. This level of consciousness should surpass every worry and care for tomorrow.

Not long after, many mind-boggling events will take place, which will cause men's hearts to fail for fear. Some will be on the verge of giving up their lives because they think it's not worth living anymore. Nonetheless, the people who do know their God will not be dismayed. Instead, they will exploit and plunder. [Daniel 11:32]. Fear is not an option for children of God in the Last Days. The Bible said that the fearful and unbelieving shall have their part in the lake of fire. Knowing that we possess the Spirit of power, love, and a sound mind, we should move forward as militants endeavoring to accomplish a mission. We should be able to look beyond the present and see what's over on the other side.

God gave me a vision of the last days not long after I got saved. This vision was dated January 11[th,] 1995. The vision was written thus:

It was as if I was in a church, and everyone was worshipping God. The next thing I was on a journey with one of my siblings. As we were walking, we started witnessing to people we met along the way- telling them about the gospel of Jesus Christ. Then, it seemed like I was headed to the top of a hill. Before reaching the top, I could sense a spirit of violence in the region. Instantly, I saw three schoolboys (preteens) stabbing at each other with sharpened lead pencils. As they stabbed each other, I saw the blood dripping from their hands. When I reached the mount and looked around, there was fire everywhere. Then the scenery changed, and I saw people crying and screaming frantically. In this scenario, it dawned on me that something dramatic occurred (the rapture), so the individuals were left stranded or hopeless. As I watched, I observed a spirit of total frenzy and confusion.

Amidst the melee, I saw a truck blasting from the north as if the driver was possessed. As the truck came rushing from the north, it collided with a train moving simultaneously from west to east. In a split second, there was a gigantic explosion. Flames of fire raged into the air as people screamed and hollered. The majority, if not all, of the people, were calling on the name of Jesus! At the same time, I saw another spectacular event: The sun stood still (like in the days of Moses and Joshua in the wilderness) in the skies towards the west. As I looked up, it was golden, bright, and shining like never before. As the folks around me were screaming and shouting for Jesus, I, too, found myself calling upon Jesus.

Then I realized I wasn't alone, for I heard a voice within me saying: "Aren't you saved? Why are you shouting?" I closed my mouth instantly and crept away from that awful scene. The next thing I know, I immediately woke up from my dream.

When I awoke, my clothing was soaked with cold sweat, as if I was in a pouring rain! I might have pinched myself to see if I was in real-time! I then crawled off the bed (trembling with fear) and to my knees.

The closing of the last days is imminent. That dream was only one of many that the Lord showed me. This was almost twenty-nine years ago. It would seem like a long time, but first, we must look at this from God's perspective regarding time. The apostle Peter declares that a thousand (earthly) years is like one day to God. This is also confirmed in the book of the Psalms: [2 Peter 3:8 and Psalm 90:4]. I refer to these scriptures to say that these dreams were given only a few seconds ago, according to God's time clock! This means that God has a set time for unfolding events under heaven, and the time is closing in rapidly.

While many think they have enough time to galvanize before settling down and surrendering their lives to Jesus Christ, time is rushing by furiously. One of the enemy's most effective weapons against humanity is to get them into unnecessary and irrelevant activities that waste their time. The cares of life are consuming so many today that they don't even realize that amid life, there is death. Yes, my friend, there is one out there seeking to kill, steal, and destroy- and that is the devil called Satan. Thus, to be covered under the mighty name of Jesus Christ through His blood is of paramount importance! I have heavily emphasized this because of my experience with God. In this contemporary world, we need God's protection. Outside of God is like living dangerously. I am not saying that lightly because viewing a house from the inside and the outside are different scenarios.

A player on a soccer field cannot see a fantastic play more clearly than a spectator off the field. However, if they trade places, the player will see the mistakes and how easy it would have been if he had played otherwise. The days are rapidly upon us; It's just a matter of time before many realize they have run out of time! The prophet Isaiah told us precisely what to do:

Seek ye the LORD while He may be found, call ye upon him while He is near: let the wicked forsake his way, and the unrighteous man

His thoughts: and let Him return unto the LORD, and He will have
mercy upon Him; and to our God, for He will abundantly pardon.

ISAIAH 55-7

Surrendering to God while we are alive and in our soundness of minds is the key to everlasting joy and contentment.

Feelings of happiness, joy, peace, and contentment come from Almighty God. Now imagine if He would pull the plug on all these emotions; the result would be catastrophic! Again, only He could be God, for if it wasn't for His gift of free will to humanity, many wouldn't be basking in the pleasures of a sinful lifestyle right now. However, this is only temporary, seeing that God will bring everything into judgment on the Last Day. Nothing will escape; judgment is inevitable, whether you are dead or alive then.

Wherefore we labour, that, whether present or absent, we may be
accepted of Him. For we shall all appear before the judgment seat
of Christ; that everyone may receive the things done in his body,
according to what he hath done, whether good or bad.

2 CORINTHIANS 5: 9-10

The Clock is ticking away; Surely, we are drawing near the hour. Every day won't be the same. That Day will come. Are you ready for the breaking of the day? One day, the busy schedule will be interrupted abruptly. There will be a snatching away of the church the bride of Christ. Wouldn't you like to be a part of this family if you are not yet involved? Looking around us, we can all see heartache and pain. Many are contemplating suicide, as you read. However, God didn't make humanity undergo such pressure, pain, and woe. His intent was for us to be prosperous and in good health. The proper knowledge of the Truth can make a significant difference in an individual's life. Many people act the way they do, often because of their thought processes. If light is shed in the direction of the mind, then the mentality will be different.

In addition, even though the proper knowledge may be obtained, it will be challenging to exercise and maintain it. That's one of the main reasons the Holy Spirit is important in our lives. Trying to balance life and stay afloat without God in a world filled with wickedness is like signing up for a suicide mission! The hard fact of life is that no one wins without God. Moreover, death is not an escape route. The result only brings us closer to God and the judgment seat. When I started writing this book, I didn't know where to begin or what to write about besides my life experience. All I knew was that God was prompting me to write. The minute I began to write, He started filling my mind with thoughts! This is the reason why I emphasize so much on spiritual things. I realized gradually that although this book was about the challenges I faced in life and how God keeps and sustains me, It's not about me but about Him!

I give God all the glory, honor, and praises due unto His name, for at the end of the day, He remains the big picture. Many today are still searching for solutions to life's issues, pain, and woes. However, Jesus remains the only answer. When a manufacturer creates a motor, for example, a vehicle, that manufacturer or company has the software blueprint for that specific vehicle. Suppose there is any issue with that vehicle; for instance, a defect is discovered. In that case, the individual in possession of the vehicle must refer back to the manufacturer, who has the blueprint for the vehicle. If that individual tries to figure it out by themselves or by others outside the scope of the manufacturer, they might cause more damage to the vehicle, and if they have had a quick fix 'thing' done on it, it won't last.

We have never seen a self-repair vehicle before, though that may be in the making. However, many of us are trying to fix our lives without Jesus, the manufacturer. We pretend to be ignorant of His pre-eminence and go about our lives, living in frustration and misery. Most of us excuse is: "We can't see God, so we are unsure if He is there." Nevertheless, in a desperate situation, we would frantically call on His name as if there is no tomorrow!

When He rescued us from that situation, though we are pretty much aware of His deliverance, we would pretend that nothing happened and that He didn't exist. Do you see how hypocritical we can become despite God's grace and mercy?

If you have experienced God's grace and mercy today, do not hesitate to receive Him into your heart. It may be your last time!

Almighty God is too good to all of us (believers and unbelievers alike) to be taken for granted. Yes, I speak for all of us; why? Because all of us have experienced God's goodness at one point or another- Even if we didn't care to give Him credit, He came through for us. Now, God does not only want to help us, but He desires for us to have sweet fellowship with Him. Whenever you hear the voice of God speaking to your heart, turn Him not away but invite Him in and thank Him for His grace and mercy and for being mindful of you. Someone would say, "How do I know it's God speaking to me?"

There are three distinct voices that we would likely to hear: Your conscience or your inner man counseling you; the voice of God encouraging and advising you into all good, positive, and divine things; And the voice of the Devil that opposes all things that are good, righteous and positive. We can always detect the enemy's voice, which can sometimes be subtle. He would be aware of things God has in store for us and encourage us to rush and attain it before God's appointed time. The Devil will influence us to do things that we know will indeed cause harmful results to us and others. No wonder the scriptures warned us about our hearts:

Keep your heart with all diligence; For out of it are the issues of life.

PROVERBS 4:23

In other words, the Scripture says that we should be careful or be aware of what comes out of our hearts because what comes out of it will be the result of a matter. Whenever we hear the voice of the Devil, we should instantly rebuke him. Listening to negative voices can lead to harming others and, ultimately, self-destruction.

These last few days, many negative voices have been ringing in the ears of many individuals. Some are even driven into insanity because they seem to have no control over these tormenting voices.

He that hath no rule over his own spirit is like a city broken down and without walls.

PROVERBS 25:28

We can take back control of our lives if we listen to the right voice, God's still and gentle voice, beckoning us to choose Him and all His righteousness.

CHAPTER 20
THE REPLENISHMENT

In a world teetering on the brink of environmental, social, and spiritual crises, the prophecy of a new Heaven and new Earth emerges as a beacon of hope. This divine intervention, foretold through ages, speaks of a moment when the fabric of reality will shift—when Jesus Christ returns to Earth, not as a savior from sins alone but as a restorer of creation itself. "The Replenishment" is a renewal of the Earth's withered veins and a promise of a new dawn for humanity, a rebirth of spirit, community, and the natural world. On that note, let us explore this profound transformation, weaving through the tapestry of biblical promises, theological insights, and the envisioned future of our world reborn. As we embark on this journey, we invite readers to imagine the possibilities of a restored Earth and to reflect on the role each can play in nurturing this hope into fruition.

In the Holy Scriptures, the book of Revelation [Revelation 21:1] states that a new heaven and a new earth will appear, for the former has vanished. To many, this would seem like the biggest miracle yet to be performed by the Almighty God. Many of us have heard and even seen miracles, signs, and wonders performed by the hands of God. But there is a need to replenish the earth by removing the old world and heaven (by refining fire) and establishing new ones we have never heard of. So, you see, our God is at it again! He has replenished the earth before through water or a destructive flood. This time, it would not be by flood but by fire! [2 Peter 3:1012].

In its current state, our world stands as a testament to both the marvels of human achievement and the grave consequences of our actions. The environment groans under the weight of pollution, deforestation, and climate change, with species disappearing at an alarming rate and natural disasters becoming increasingly severe and frequent. Socially, divisions run deep as inequality, conflict, and injustice fracture communities and nations. Spiritually, a sense of disconnection pervades, with many feeling lost in pursuing material satisfaction, yearning for a deeper understanding of purpose and connection.

Nevertheless, the replenishment of this world is inevitable. Since the fall of man, the whole creation has been under pressure. Not only did the curse affect man and beast but the entire world alike. However, God's ultimate divine plan soon comes to full fruition. The concept of divine judgment and the subsequent creation of a new Heaven and Earth are foundational to the predominantly Christian community and have captivated the human imagination for centuries. To be sure that a divine judgment is inevitable, we must always focus on the signs around us. Before the replenishment, several events must occur, along with certain prophetic utterances that God imparted to His ministers and prophets of old. The book of Revelation, often cited as the most direct scriptural source regarding the end times, details events leading up to and including God's final judgment- symbols like the Four Horsemen, the Beast, and the judgment of the dead are all expounded here.

The Book of Daniel also offers visions and prophecies that have been interpreted as predictions of the end times, including the rise and fall of empires and the ultimate sovereignty of God. Now, in the book of Matthew 24, Jesus discusses the end of the age with His disciples, describing signs and events that would precede His second coming and the final judgment. In many religious teachings today, a decline in moral and social values signals the approach of the end times. Issues such as widespread dishonesty, loss of integrity, gross deception, and diminishing respect for life are often displayed. They stare us down daily as we inch toward the end of time.

Increasing acceptance of behaviors traditionally viewed as immoral or unethical by various religious doctrines can also be seen as signs of the times. This includes debates on marriage, family structures, and human rights.

The constant threat of climatic depletion, unprecedented natural disasters, and the degradation of natural resources are often paralleled with scriptural prophecies about the Earth's suffering in the last days. Other signs of the time, such as blood moons, solar eclipses, and comets, are sometimes interpreted by believers as the beginning or the end of the time mentioned in the Holy Scriptures. As we get closer to the end, the rapid advancement of technology and changes in global politics are also displayed before us, assuring us of the fulfillment of prophecies. Developments like artificial intelligence, surveillance, and the digital economy raise concerns that align with prophetic themes of absolute control and the mark of the beast. Now, the rise of globalism shifts towards one-world government structures, and international coalitions are sometimes interpreted through the lens of prophecy, suggesting a setting stage for the prophesied global leader or antichrist.

Now, the snatching away (which is known as the Rapture) of the church must take place before 'hell' is let loose on earth. [1 Corinthians 15:51-52, 2 Thessalonians 2:7]. Yes, my friend, this gospel teaching is not to intimidate anyone but for you to turn your attention to Him, God. Moreover, if you are not already dismayed by what's happening here, I don't know what else should make you be. As for me, I have seen enough that makes me want to say, "Amen, even so, come Lord Jesus"! However, after the Rapture (the snatching away of the church), the tribulation period that was spoken of in the Bible will begin. This will include wars, famines, plagues, diseases, and natural disasters as precursors to God's direct intervention. With all these happenings unfolding here on earth, let me ask you, my friend, are you ready? If the question is unclear, let me ask again- are you ready to meet your God? Believe it or not, He is about to show up shortly. The signs are everywhere!

The Millennial dispensation is about to begin, and the church era is on the verge of ending. God is not a man that He should lie; Neither is He a God that fails. However, before the replenishment, several events will unfold. Firstly, the church will be raptured, the tribulation era will begin (the anti-Christ will appear, enforcing the mark of the beast), and then Jesus will return with His bride (the raptured church) and with the army of heaven. The holy scriptures declare that all eyes shall behold Him, even those that pierced Him. Now, this is where the first resurrection takes place. Those martyred because they rejected the antichrist and his mark will be resurrected, including those whom God sees fit to enter because of their righteousness or good deeds in their era or dispensation.

However, in this era of the church or the dispensation of grace, the only way to be saved is through the blood of Jesus Christ of Nazareth. This is the era where we must be baptized in Jesus' name and filled with the Holy Ghost to make it into the kingdom of God. Yes, my friend, there is no other way out. The Replenishment is about to begin. Men have been trying for the longest time to make the world a better place to inhabit effectively but without success. They have advanced technology today that can influence or manipulate weather conditions but still can't get it right. Instead of fixing the earth's problem, they only cause more complexity and confusion.

The world's problems and solutions are in the hands of Almighty God, the creator of all things. If we take Him out of the equation, the whole functionality of life itself would be lopsided. That is one of, if not the most paramount, why Jesus came.

For God so loved the world, that He gave His only begotten son, that whosoever believeth in Him should not perish, but have everlasting life.

JOHN 3:16

The world's problems cannot be fixed while the opposer and adversary of our souls still exist. Chaos and disorder will prevail if this culprit is still in the big picture. The Bible states that Satan will be bound and cast into the lake of fire, and that will be the end of his reckless pursuit to destroy the world, including humanity. [Revelation 20:10].

A new heaven and earth are in view. The word of God declares that the eye has not seen, the ear has not heard, and neither has it entered into the heart of man, the things that God has prepared for them, that love Him. During the replenishment, we will receive a new body. Everything will be new! Moreover, there will be a lot of changes, of course not for the worse but for the better and joy of God's people. If you can now, only imagine; soon, it will be a reality! God is faithful that promised. God being who He is, anything He says will happen. Anything He planned will be fulfilled. It will happen if He must change the weather, time, or circumstances. God is not a man that He should lie. [Numbers 23: 19].

Many people's minds are often blown when they try to figure out how God will bring a specific thing to pass or whether He has that potential. This is where men get in trouble with God—by questioning his capability.

> *Behold I am the Lord, the God of all flesh: is there anything too hard for me?*

> JEREMIAH 32:27

God becomes extremely displeased when we allow doubt and fear to creep into our lives and not trust Him. The man who was in charge of the king's affairs at the time of the siege in Jerusalem responded to the prophecy of the prophet sarcastically to show his distaste and unbelief: " Then Elisha said, hear ye the word of the Lord; Thus saith the Lord, tomorrow about this time shall a measure of fine flour be sold for a shekel, and two measures of barley for a shekel, in the gate of Samaria.

Then a lord on whose hand the king leaned answered the man of God and said, Behold, if the Lord would make windows in heaven, might this thing be?" Elijah replied, "Behold thou shalt see it with thine eyes, but shalt not eat thereof." What took place next was nothing short of amazing. God did a miraculous work to prove that He is a provider. Israel was fed, but unfortunately, as Elisha had prophesied, the man didn't live to partake of the blessings. "And the people went out and spoiled the tents of the Syrians. So, a measure of fine flour was sold for a shekel and two measures of barley for a shekel, according to the word of the Lord. And the king appointed the lord on whose hand he leaned to have charge of the gate:

And the people trode upon him in the gate, and he died, as the man of God had said, who spake when the king came down to him. And it came to pass as the man of God had spoken to the king, saying, Two measure of barley for a shekel, and a measure of fine flour for a shekel, shall be to morrow about this time in the gate of Samaria: and the lord answered the man of God, and said, Now, behold, if the Lord should make windows in heaven, might such a thing be? And he said, Behold, thou shalt see it with thine eyes, but shalt not eat thereof. And so it fell out unto him: for the people trode upon him in the gate, and he died.

2 KINGS 7:17-20

Have you been sarcastic about the word of God- or any prophecy spoken over your life by a real man of God?

If so, then repent immediately. Almighty God is not mock; whatever a man sows, that he shall also reap. Even if you have ever held any form of doubt, give God the benefits. He can't do anything for you if you always have doubt creeping over your shoulder. God promised to get rid of the old nature of this world and replace it with a mind-blowing one! Do you believe it? Are you in sync with His word? The word of God declares that this world will pass away and its lusts, but whosoever shall obey God's 'Will' will live forever! [1 John 2: 17]. Wow! What a promise! Suppose at one point in our lives, God made us a promise; we waited long enough for it but received something else. In that case, it can be either of two things: It wasn't God (that's when we ask amiss and expect something that never happen), or we somehow got messed up along the way and thus missed the promise.

Most of us know the Scripture that says nothing good will He withhold from them that walk uprightly. That does not necessarily mean that what we deem good is good for us in God's sight. Like a parent relating to their child, He knows that certain things, if granted to us, will harm our spiritual walk. For example, a gambler who has never handled a certain amount of money suddenly hits the jackpot. He started buying and doing stuff that was not even necessary or good for his well-being, such as drugs, booze, throwing wild parties, and such. Eventually, he soon grew broke, and his health deteriorated. That doesn't mean that a child of God would follow suit. However, God knows what's best for us individually and what would not turn our hearts away from Him.

Often, we observe that a man's life does not consist of the abundance of things he can hoard. We have seen and heard of so-called wealthy and famous individuals who die and leave all their precious substances behind. Unfortunately, they couldn't take what they possessed with them. Solomon, the wisest king in the Holy Scriptures, describes it as vanity and vexation of spirit.

> *There is one alone, and there is not a second; yea, he hath neither child nor brother: yet is there no end to his labour; neither is his eyes satisfied with riches; neither saith he, For whom do I labour, and bereave my soul of good? This is also vanity, yea it is a sore travail.*

ECCLESIASTES 4: 8

Moreover, the things we possess below cannot be compared with the things that Jesus Christ has gone to prepare for those who love Him. The replenishment is one of amazement.

> *But as it is written, eye hath not seen, nor ear heard, neither have it entered into the heart of man, the things which God hath prepared for them that love Him.*

1 CORINTHIANS 2: 9

There you have it. The Scripture suggested that we cannot even come close to imagining heaven's great splendor and majestical wonder.

The overall changes in the whole universe will be phenomenal. We will no longer need things like the sun, the moon, and night itself. God Himself shall be the light for His people.

> *And He shewed me a pure river of water of life, clear as crystal, proceeding out of the throne of God and of the Lamb. In the midst of the street of it, and on either side of the river, was there the tree of life, which bare twelve manner of fruits, and yielded her fruit every month: and the leaves of the tree were for the healing of the nations. And there shall no more curse: but the throne of God and of the Lamb shall be in it; and his servants shall serve Him. And they shall see His face; and His name shall be in their foreheads. And there shall be no night there; and they need no candle, neither light of the sun, for the Lord God giveth them light: and they shall reign for ever and ever.*

REVELATION 22: 1

Yes, my friend, the replenishment is about to happen. Will you be a part of this significant event that will be taking place in heaven, or have you decided otherwise?

There was a man of the Pharisees named Nicodemus, who came to Jesus by night. He didn't want anyone to see him (especially his Sanhedrin associates) enquiring about someone his brethren hated and already rejected, so he disguised himself in the shadows. Sometimes, an individual wants to encounter God, but hindrances such as friends, families, status, and possessions prevent them. Out of desperation, that individual would go out of their way to have that one-on-one experience with God. If you need Him, you will find Him. Nicodemus was a little anxious because of what he saw, thought, and heard about Jesus. He knew something different about this man of God, so his conscience wouldn't let up. When he saw Jesus, he had no choice but to confess how he felt about Him, and Jesus, in turn, gave him the formula of how to be saved.

> *Jesus answered and said unto him. Verily verily I say unto thee, except a man be born again, he cannot see the kingdom of God. Nicodemus saith unto Him, How can a man be born when he is old? Can he enter the second time into his mother's womb and be born? Jesus answered, verily, verily, I say unto thee, except a man be born of the water and of the Spirit, he cannot enter into the kingdom of God. That which is born of the flesh is flesh, and that which is born of the Spirit is spirit. Marvel not that I said unto thee, ye must be born again.*

> JOHN 3: 5-7

Humanity must be prepared to meet their God before the replenishment. We cannot be transported to that new heaven in our old adamic state or nature. As Jesus suggested to Nicodemus, we must be born again of the water, the spirit, and the blood. "Why is this important?" one may ask. "Why did Adam and Eve need to obey God's instruction? "Simply because there are consequences in disobeying the commandments of God. For instance, as a result of disobedience, Adam and Eve were driven from the Garden of Eden, and punishment was pronounced on everyone involved in violating God's instruction. However, God gave them hope through the seed of the woman, who will ultimately crush the head of the serpent.

There is something far more significant than death, my friend, and it is the Afterlife or Eternity. Are you ready? Eternity means what it is- everlasting, which means everything continues in its present state forever. Once an individual soul transits into eternity, there is no going back. That is it! Wherever the tree falls there, it will be until the property owner decides where it should go. We only live once here on earth, but there is a permanent place prepared by Almighty God for everyone, according to our deeds on earth. No one is exempt from the judgment that is to come. To live in God's presence forever, we must abide by His commands. There will be no rebels in the presence of God. No one who opposes God's rules and ordinances will be in His presence. There is a place for rebels, designed originally for the devil and his angels. However, since some individuals decided to follow suit (that is, rebelling against God with no hope of repenting), they will also be cast into a devil's hell. This may seem harsh to many, but God is sovereign, and what He says stands forever. Moreover, His commandments are not grievous. When an individual walks in the ways of the LORD, it's impossible for them not to experience unspeakable joy and glory influenced by the Holy Ghost that lives within.

When an individual comes to Christ, they can never be the same again! This is because the spiritual birth brings them to another level of experience with God. Old things indeed are passed away, and all things become new! Who wouldn't like to experience such a change? The long and tiresome years of being in the norm and sin have caused many folks to be disinterested in a change. Some would even think aloud when they heard about salvation and a change of heart toward godliness- "I am not used to that; this is what I am used to, and I am sticking to it." -They would echo.

However, despite some rejecting this full and free salvation, it does not change God's will and intention regarding this world and man's life. Many are excited, while others are uncertain of their standing with God. Some have gone before without the blessed hope, while many have gone rejoicing. There is a gospel hymnal whose chorus goes like this:

Oh, I want to see Him, to look upon His face, there to sing forever, of His saving grace, on the street of glory, let me lift my voice, care's all past, home at last, ever to rejoice!

Can you imagine what a moment that will be? I am already getting excited!

For God hath not appointed us to wrath, but to obtain salvation by our Lord Jesus Christ, who died for us, that, whether we wake or sleep, we should live together with him. Wherefore comfort yourselves together, and edify one another, even as also ye do.

1 THESSALONIANS 5:9

Indeed, God will be coming to replenish the Earth and to establish his kingdom. All eyes will see Him as He descended with the church (His bride) and the army of heaven. It is as real as the day is from the night and will happen as He promised. The ruler of this present world is the prince of darkness, and he will be dethroned shortly. He will be bound and cast into the bottomless pit, a place of restriction. All disobedient and unrighteous individuals will also be cast into this horrible place:

And the devil that deceived them was cast into the lake of fire and brimstone, where the beast and the false prophet are, and shall be tormented day and night forever and ever.

REVELATION 20:10

Yes, my friend, God will surely fulfill His promise, and not one title of His word shall fail. A new heaven and a new earth are on the horizon. There will be a significant change. There will be no more sea or dangerous sea creatures anymore. There will be a new and holy city, the new Jerusalem. Amen.

ABOUT THE AUTHOR
HOWARD A BLAKE: A MULTIFACETED LIFE OF SERVICE AND COMMITMENT

EARLY LIFE AND BACKGROUND:

Howard A. Blake was born in the rural area of Kingston, Jamaica. He was born again (spiritually) in the Ebenezer Pentecostal Church in 1994 before migrating to the United States of America in 1999. He has recently started a branch of the Ebenezer Pentecostal Church called 'The Mount Gerezim Ebenezer Pentecostal.' From an early age, it was clear that Howard was destined for a path that intertwined his spiritual beliefs, entrepreneurial spirit, and literary talents.

SPIRITUAL LEADERSHIP:

Howard's unwavering commitment to his faith led him to become an Elder in his local church in South Florida. His deep understanding of biblical teachings and ability to connect with people on a personal level quickly made him a respected figure in his congregation. He has mentored young church members and adults alike, providing spiritual guidance and encouragement to willing listeners. Howard's infectious enthusiasm and compassionate approach made him a beloved pillar of his church community.

PREACHING WITH PASSION:

In addition to his role as an elder, Howard took up the preacher's mantle. His sermons were known for their profound insights, relatable anecdotes, and unwavering passion for conveying the word of God. Howard's ability to break down complex theological concepts into understandable and relatable messages drew people from all walks of life to his sermons. His powerful oratory skills and magnetic presence turned each sermon into an unforgettable spiritual experience.

LITERARY PURSUITS:

Beyond his roles as a preacher and realtor, Howard's love for writing blossomed into a successful career as a writer and author. He penned several inspirational poems and now focuses on writing books that resonate deeply with readers seeking spiritual growth, personal development, and practical life advice. His works combined personal experiences, spiritual insights, and literary prowess to create a unique and impactful voice.

A PURSUIT FOR PERFECTION:

Howard A Blake balances his numerous roles in the picturesque South Florida area with grace and dedication. His life is a testament to the power of faith, hard work, and a genuine desire to serve others. Howard's impact is far-reaching and enduring, whether he delivers a moving sermon, helps a family find their perfect home, or inspires readers with his written words. His journey inspires all who seek to live a life of purpose, compassion, and success.

In every facet of his life, Howard Abraham Blake exemplifies the qualities of a true leader, a devoted servant, and a compassionate human being. His legacy is of unwavering faith, boundless generosity, and a profound commitment to improving the world.

www.ingramcontent.com/pod-product-compliance
Lightning Source LLC
Chambersburg PA
CBHW020230130626
46549CB00005B/1826